PAUL KLEE

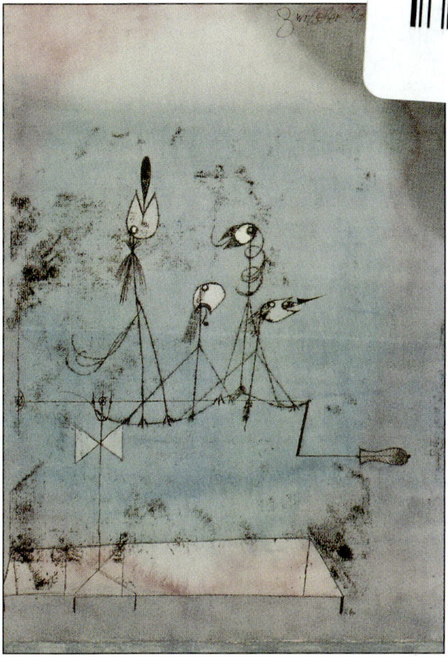

T&J

Published by TAJ Books International LLC 2013
5501 Kincross Lane
Charlotte, North Carolina, USA
28277

www.tajbooks.com
www.tajminibooks.com

All notations of errors or omissions (author inquiries, permissions) concerning the content of this book should be addressed to info@tajbooks.com.

ISBN 978-1-84406-239-3
978-1-62732-011-5 Paperback

Printed in China

2 3 4 5 17 16 15 14

PAUL KLEE

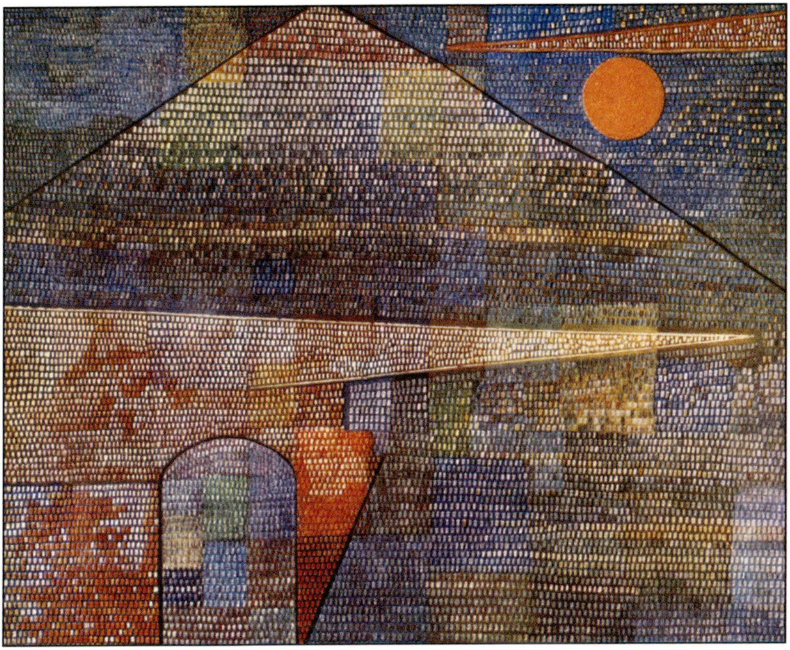

T&J

SANDRA FORTY

PAUL KLEE

1879–1940

Paul Klee's philosophy of art is perhaps best summed up by his statement: "A drawing is simply a line going for a walk."

From a very young age, Paul Klee was a talented musician, but as he grew older he realized that his true vocation lay with art. Despite this passion, it took him years of frustrating experimentation to discover his artistic "voice" and the development and fruition of his exceptional eye as a color theorist of unparalleled skill. In later years, he communicated some of his understanding to upcoming artists when he taught at the influential German Bauhaus academy in Weimar, and later in Dessau, after the academy moved in 1925. Klee's interest, understanding, and analysis of color theory and tone–which he explained in several influential books–has arguably left a greater legacy than his artworks.

As one of the great avant garde artists of the early 20th century, Klee was swept along with the changing moods and philosophies of the time. He was open to new ideas and artistic insights and experiments, welcoming inspiration from other artists, both alive and dead. This was a revolutionary time in art as unconventional artists started to explore color, technique, and sheer abstraction. The Post-Impressionists (Picasso, Braque, van Gogh, and Cézanne) led the way, to be rapidly followed by Cubists, Fauvists, German Expressionists, and many more. These movements completely revolutionized the concept of what was acceptable as art–albeit in the face of antagonism from many traditionalists.

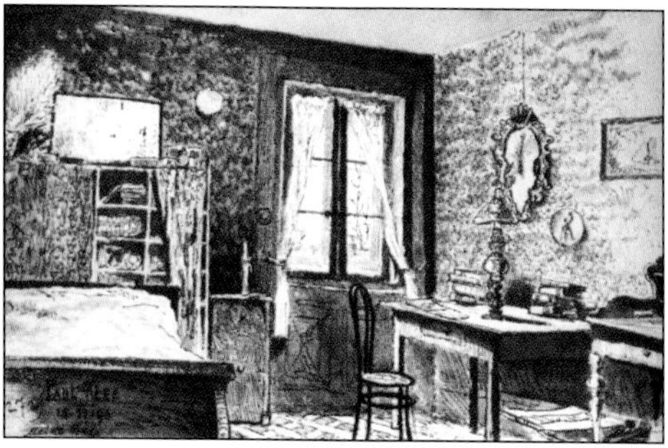

My Room (Meine Bude), 1896

Paul Klee crested this wave of innovation and experimented with many of the new approaches and techniques as he explored various ways of producing art. For Klee, the process of making art was every bit as important as the finished item. He wrote in one of his many notebooks: "The act of giving

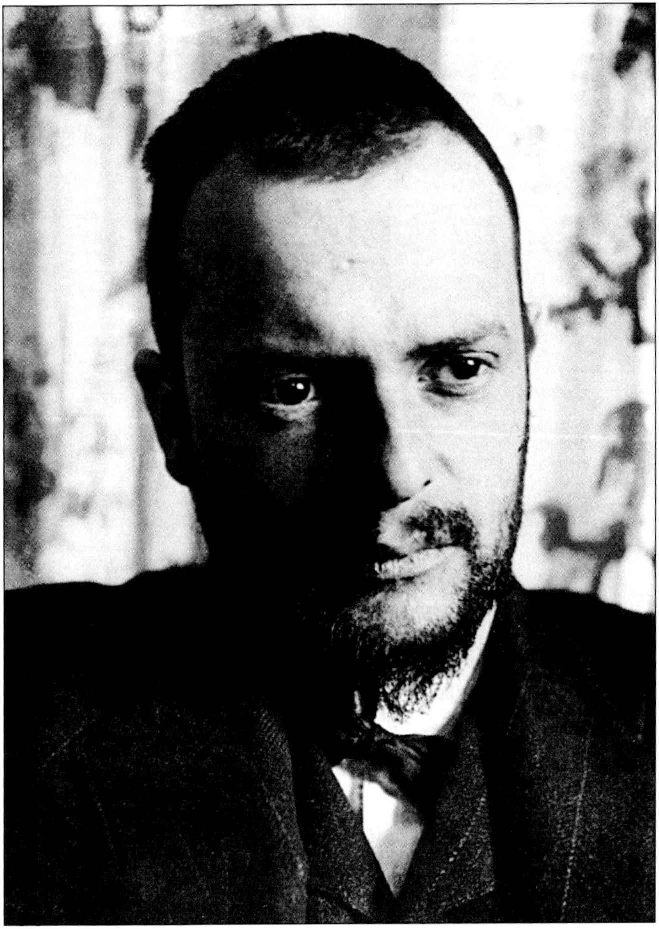

Paul Klee, 1911

form determines form itself and the process is more important than the form."

Klee was inspired by the works of other artists, freely acknowledging his reverence for Michelangelo, as well as for his near contemporaries: Cézanne, van Gogh, Picasso, Matisse, Rousseau, and Kandinsky. He was also influenced by the early modernist theories surrounding Surrealism as well as Dada and Cubism—influences he took and submerged into his own creative concepts. His philosophical approach was based on Einstein's theory of relativity. This fascinated and intrigued Klee who attempted to incorporate some of these world-changing ideas into his own work.

Klee did not readily fit into a particular artistic category. He used many styles and techniques, always exploring the different variations each media opened up to him.

When he worked, Klee channeled his mood through the process of using areas of color that he then outlined or added figures to embellish. Some of his paintings are simply color and shade studies, juxtaposing light and tone to produce a work of lyrical beauty. He said, "Color is the irrational element in painting and chief vehicle of expression." He wanted to present his works as "disciplined simplicity" in order to portray seeing the world through child-like eyes. When his work was criticized as little more than the scribbles of a child, he claimed to be delighted. By extension, he also revered the work of so-called primitive artists who perceived the world around them and re-created that world with a pure vision.

Klee's works are of an abstract or a representational nature and are created from a variety of media—in addition to oil, also watercolor, gouache, and tempera. Furthermore, his painting was often embellished by etchings and engravings. An important element in his work is the use of symbols and words to convey thoughts and philosophies directly on the canvas. These often humorous additions show his gentle wit and satirical eye.

Klee liked to think of his works as visual poetry that could be read and enjoyed for their meaning, but could also be hung on the wall. He said, "In art it is not seeing that is so important, but making visible." To provide even greater diversification, Klee habitually used a variety of surfaces on which to paint, not just conventional canvas, but linen or even fine gauze, and sometimes coarse burlap or board, glass, or any textured surface on which color could be applied.

After finishing each work, he performed a ritual: a week after completing a painting he would hold a naming ceremony for it.

A recurring image in his work is a cat—he loved animals—because Klee believed they were the essence of sensuality. In the corners and around the edges of his work, a cat is often visible. Klee was especially attached to his own cat, Bimbo, and while traveling would write to his wife to anxiously inquire about him, rather than about his wife or his son!

Klee could work with either hand, although he tended to write with his right hand, and draw and paint with his left. As an unwitting gift to art historians, between 1897 and 1918 Klee kept a diary in which he explored his ideas and ruminations on art. The diary provides a valuable insight into his thought processes during the period: "To emphasize only the beautiful seems to me to be like a mathematical system that only concerns itself with positive numbers."

Paul Klee was born in the canton of Bern, Switzerland, on December 18, 1879, in the small village of Münchenbuchsee bei Bern. His German father, Hans Klee, was a music teacher and the church organist, and although Paul was born in Switzerland he was given his father's German citizenship. His Swiss mother, Ida Marie Frick, was a former professional singer who abandoned her career when she married. The couple already had a three-year-old daughter, Mathilde, to whom Paul was very close all his life.

Klee recalled that he first started drawing when he was only three or four years old, encouraged by the colored chalks and paper supplied by his doting Swiss grandmother. Some of Klee's early drawings survive and show him attempting to capture his surroundings. His grandmother also read him fairy stories and showed him religious iconography that inspired his early drawings. Even as a child he habitually took a sketch book with him when he went to visit his relatives around Switzerland, especially to his uncle's rural restaurant where he was fascinated by the colors and swirls of the restaurant's marble table tops.

His parents, however, had other ambitions for Klee. They wanted him to follow in their footsteps and to become a professional musician. Thus, he was taught the violin from an early age. He was clearly talented and played in the local youth orchestra during his teens. Music remained one of the great loves of his life, but he did not want to make a career of it—much to the disappointment of both his parents.

As a child, Klee attended the Progymnasium in the center of Bern and then the Literarschule. Despite his obvious intelligence, he was only an average scholar. The only subject he showed any aptitude for was Greek, a love he retained throughout his life. He read Greek poetry until the day he died. Klee did not enjoy school and tried to leave early, but his parents insisted that he stay on another year. He only just managed to pass his exit exams in 1898.

Although Klee still had strong parental pressure to pursue a musical career, he was already being called to his destiny of painter and artist. To further his artistic education, he had the choice of Paris or Munich, and he chose the latter. So, just two months after leaving school, Klee left home for Munich in southern Germany. The popular and prevailing artistic movement in Munich (and Germany as a whole) was Jugendstil, a Germanic variant of Art Nouveau. In Munich, Klee joined a private school to study drawing. He had failed to get into the Munich Academy because his figure drawing was too poor. After improving his skill—and a heavy diary of socializing—he was accepted by the Academy, where one of his tutors was the celebrated Symbolist and society painter Franz von Stuck.

Over the next four years, Klee completed his artistic education in Germany. During this time, in 1901–02, he toured Italy for six months, admiring and absorbing all the art and culture he discovered there. He especially liked the early Christian and Byzantine artworks, but was much less impressed by the Renaissance artists and other later luminaries, with the exception of Michelangelo. Back in Germany, in order to supplement the small income supplied by his father, he sold topical political satirical drawings. At one of the many musical events he attended, he met and fell for Lily Stumpf, a young Bavarian pianist.

Finally, in 1902, after a four-year absence, Klee returned home to Bern to live with his parents, but he soon returned to Munich to propose to Lily. He was in no hurry to marry her though because he wanted first to fully develop as an artist. Still unable to earn a living with his painting, he earned money by playing the violin and writing the occasional theater review. All the while, he continued working hard to improve his drawing technique.

Still struggling to find his own style, Klee finally had a breakthrough over a period that culminated in 1905 and which was characterized by his satirical etching. In parallel, he had devised his own technique of drawing with a steel needle on a blackened pane of glass; he produced almost 60 drawings this way. In 1906, Klee exhibited these etchings at his first one-man show for the *Münchner Sezession* (Munich Secession). The etchings were such a critical and financial success that he no longer needed his father's help to support himself.

At last, after an four-year engagement,

Klee and Lily married in 1906. He joined her in Munich where they lived in the artists' quarter. Happily settled in Germany, Klee came into greater contact with modernist painters and eagerly soaked up their progressive ideas like a sponge. Lily gave piano lessons and Klee did the cooking and housework. The following year their son Felix was born. Klee assumed day-to-day responsibility for his young son, using the kitchen as his studio so that he could paint as well as cook the family meals and look after Felix.

In the evenings, Klee would accompany Lily on the violin while friends joined them for a few joyful hours of music, drink, and conversation. They lived a very sociable life surrounded by many friends and enjoyed numerous musical and artistic engagements and experiences.

On sunny days, Klee and Felix would sit on their balcony or go for a walk so Felix could play with toys Klee had made for him. Whenever he had the opportunity, Klee took Felix to Bern to visit his parents. The two of them regularly made the trip, often staying for a number of weeks at a time. Meanwhile, Lily remained in Munich giving lessons. With Felix safely under grandparental care, Klee was free to wander around Switzerland drawing and sketching as the mood took him.

In 1907, Klee met and befriended many notable artists such as Franz Marc, Alexei Jawlensky, August Macke, and in particular, Vasily Kandinsky, with whom he formed a life-long friendship. Klee began exhibiting his works in Munich and Berlin alongside his new artist friends and started to make a name for himself as an artist to watch. In 1911, he was noticed by a wider public through his philosophical illustrations for an edition of Voltaire's *Candide.*

That same year Klee became a member of the Russo/German Fauvist- and Cubist-influenced *Der Blaue Reiter* (The Blue Rider) art group along with Kandinsky, Franz Marc, Alexei Jawlensky, Lionel Feininger, and others. Their primary philosophy was that powerful emotions could be expressed and aroused by color alone, which produced the "stirring of the human spirit to which in the past only music had been free to do justice." The group was forced to break up in 1914 when World War I started. Marc and Macke were both killed in the early years of the war, and the Russian members were forced to return to Russia.

In 1912, a large van Gogh exhibition was held in Munich showcasing his letters as well as his paintings and drawings. Klee was immensely struck by van Gogh's vivid, highly emotional style, and declared him a genius: "This is a brain which is suffering from the burning fire of a star." He was so excited by the Post-Impressionist art that he journeyed to Paris to see for himself the works of the leading Cubists: Pablo Picasso and Georges Braque. He also met Robert Delaunay at his studio and became greatly influenced by his approach to color. Klee returned to Munich with a new passion to explore tonality in his own work.

Also around 1912, Klee became strongly interested in the Expressionist ideas behind *Der Sturm* (*The Storm*), a weekly magazine that was published between 1914 and 1932 to celebrate modern art and literature in Germany. Klee at this time was occasionally teaching, and he was very good at it. Explaining the theories behind his work helped him analyze his paintings and make progress in his own art. As a teacher, he thought of himself as a guide, helping his students discover their abilities for themselves, not a master telling them what to do.

When World War I broke out, Klee, a German citizen, was called to enlist in the German army. But with the intervention of Ludwig III, King of Bavaria, artists were exempted from active service. As a consequence, Klee's war work was divided between painting camouflage on aircraft used by the Imperial German Army, clerking in a paymaster's office, and accompanying military transports to the front. During this period he mostly painted small, rather intimate watercolors.

Soon after the war ended, Klee visited Tunisia in North Africa where he was stunned and dazzled by the light and color. It was a life-changing trip that entirely revolutionized his attitude and ideas surrounding his relationship with color and form. He said, "Color has taken possession of me; no longer do I have to chase after it, I know that it has hold of me forever. . . Color and I are one. I am a painter." As a result he started making brilliant paintings composed of colored squares singing across his canvas.

By now Paul Klee was a highly respected and successful artist and a leading light of the Modernist movement in Germany. As a consequence, in 1920, he was invited by Walter Gropius to join the teaching roster at his prestigious Bauhaus school in Munich.

The Bauhaus in Weimar was the leading international Modernist art school where the teaching emphasized the synergy between art and craft to produce functional art and architecture for the masses. The academy included artists, writers, architects, and musicians with the intent of combining their talents to throw over the old and establish a

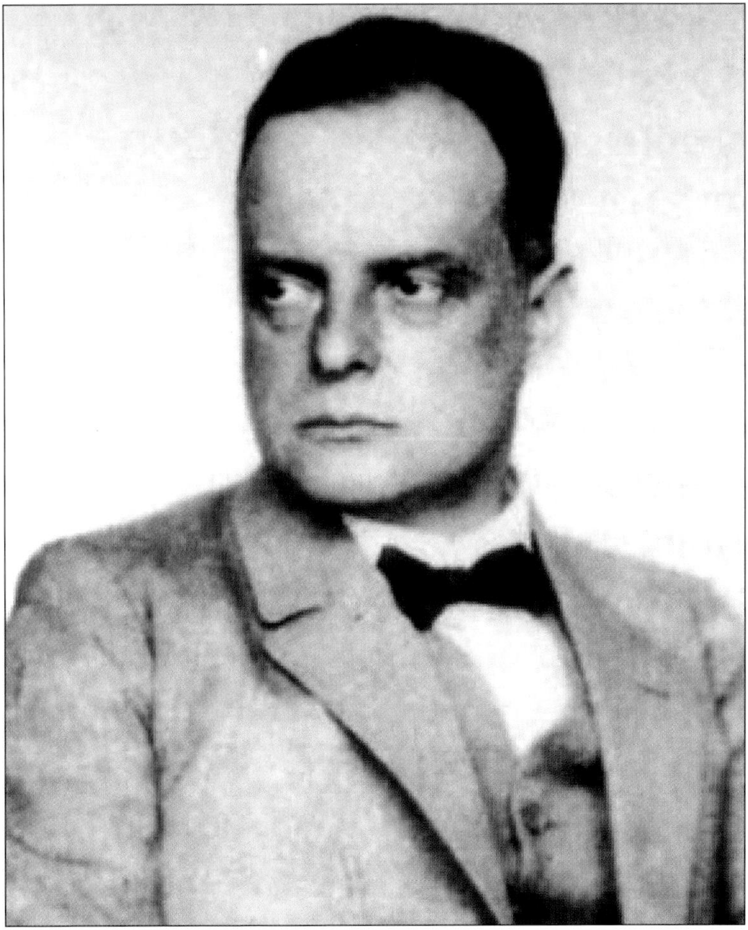

Paul Klee, 1927

new formula for creating order and function in art and architecture so that everyone could benefit from their improvements. Bauhaus philosophy and teachings proved massively influential for furniture design and architecture.

Klee loved the work and reveled in the shared thoughts and explorations of other luminaries coming together from many artistic disciplines. When the Bauhaus moved to Dessau in Germany, Klee and Kandinsky shared a studio, and their families shared a large Gropius-designed faculty house. The two friends also shared a love of color and music, which they both suffused into their work.

Klee's mother, Ida, died in 1921, 15 years after becoming partially paralyzed. Mother and son had become so close during her long years of illness that on the day she died, Klee dreamed of a female ghost floating through his studio.

While teaching at the Bauhaus in 1923, Klee—along with Kandinsky, Feininger, and Jawlensky—formed *Die Blaue Vier* (The Blue Four). All except Jawlensky were lecturers at the Bauhaus. The following year, they exhibited and lectured in the United States. The American-born Feininger summed up his friend Klee in this way: "Klee the painter is unthinkable without Klee the musician."

During these years, Klee was very productive and created some of his most famous works. Most notably, he devised his magic squares. Loosely based on a mathematical grid structure, they are progressive rhythmic chromatic studies of color pigments. Through these works, he was attempting to solve a challenging intellectual problem; he was trying to interweave art and poetry with mathematics and mysticism to create a uniquely personal statement. These challenges absorbed him more and more until he started to drop the number of classes he was teaching. His colleagues, however, some of whom the extra workload fell on, were not as enamored as Klee with his intellectual explorations, and they complained bitterly. Finally, giving in to peer pressure, Klee resigned from his position and moved to Düsseldorf to teach at the state-run Düsseldorf Art Academy, where he stayed for two years.

In 1927, the National Socialist Society for German Culture was formed with the intent of promoting Aryan art and halting the modernist "corruption of art." Increasing pressure was put on the Bauhaus to close. During the late 1920s and early 1930s, National Socialism gained political control of Germany, and in 1933, the Nazi Party came to power. The Nazis inherently suspected all artists and writers of sedition, particularly those who aligned themselves with Modernist ideas. Such people were condemned by the regime as "degenerate" and unwelcome even in their own homeland. The Bauhaus school felt the force of the Nazis' displeasure, and a few months after Klee left, the school was forced to close.

Now a state employee, Klee was forced along with everyone else to prove his Aryan antecedents on penalty of losing his job. He wanted to keep his post and went about getting the supporting documents, even though he despised the Nazis. But while he was in the process of sorting out all the paperwork, the Nazis suddenly announced that the documentation had to be accompanied by a declaration of loyalty to Hitler and the Nazi Party. Klee refused and, as a result, lost his job. Suddenly it was too dangerous for him to remain in Germany. He fled back to Bern in December 1933 at the same time his works were being removed from public galleries across Germany.

In 1937, all galleries, museums, and public areas in Germany were purged of "degenerate" art. To emphasize their point, 650 of the "worst" examples were collected and exhibited as *Entartete Kunst* (Degenerate Art) in 12 cities around Germany and Austria, starting in Munich. The hanging made it clear what the regime thought of the works: graffiti unsubtly reviling and jeering at the art accompanied it. A number of Klee's works were included alongside those of his friend Kandinsky and other luminaries, such as Max Ernst and Marc Chagall.

Klee and Lily found a two-bedroom flat in Bern in Kistlerweg, in the leafy Elfenau quarter. But Klee's health was deteriorating, and in 1935, he was showing the first signs of scleroderma, a chronic immune disease that primarily affects the skin but can also progress to the major organs, although the diagnosis was not made until after his death. His health was so bad in 1936 that he only painted 25 works of art rather than his usual hundreds. As Klee became physically more uncomfortable, his paintings grew more somber–after all, he was a mood painter. His pictures became literally darker and they entertained the themes of war, death, and destruction. He entered a string of sanitariums in an attempt to regain his health, but to no avail. For many years he had tried to get Swiss citizenship. Sadly, he died just six days before it was granted.

Paul Klee died at the age of 60 on June 29, 1940, in Muralto-Locarno, Switzerland. He left a legacy of almost 9,000 pieces of art as well as his poetry and diaries. The art consists of almost 4,000 paintings and over 5,000 works on paper. Klee was cremated. Lily kept his ashes in an urn until her death when they were interred together at Schosshaldenfriedhof, in Bern.

Their son Felix wrote the words for their tombstone: "I belong not only to this life. I live well with the dead, as well as those unborn. Nearer to the heart of creation than others. But still not close enough."

Plate 1

CAT WITH GINGER BOOTS LICKING ITSELF

1905, Zentrum Paul Klee, Bern, Switzerland
18 x 13 cm, Reverse glass painting

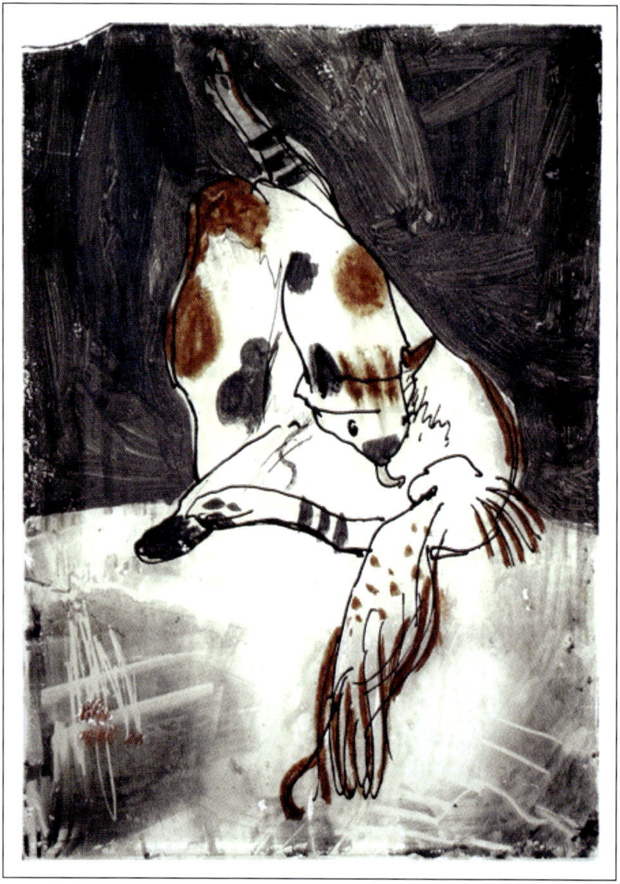

NUDE ON A SWING

1906, Zentrum Paul Klee, Bern, Switzerland
24 x 16 cm, Reverse glass painting

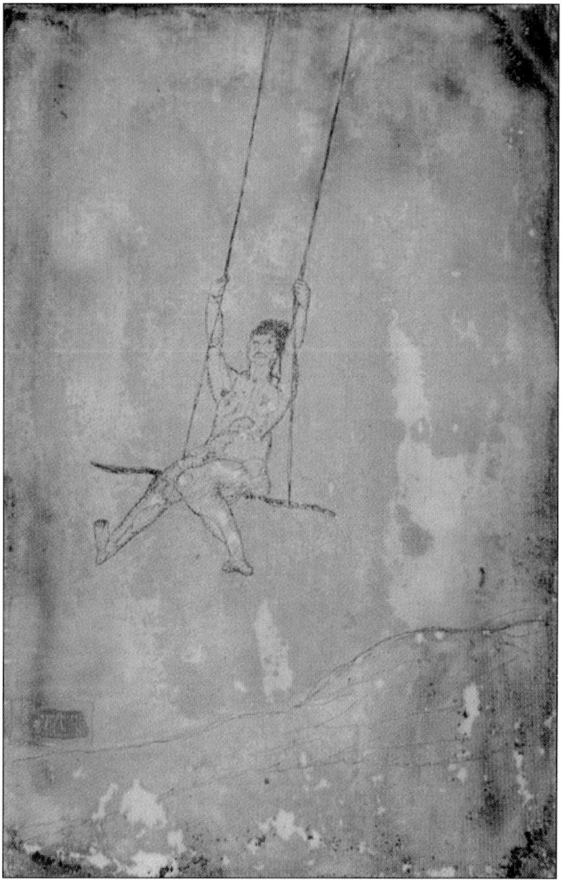

Plate 3

PORTRAIT OF AN EMOTIONAL LADY

1907, Zentrum Paul Klee, Bern, Switzerland

24 x 15.8 cm, Reverse glass painting

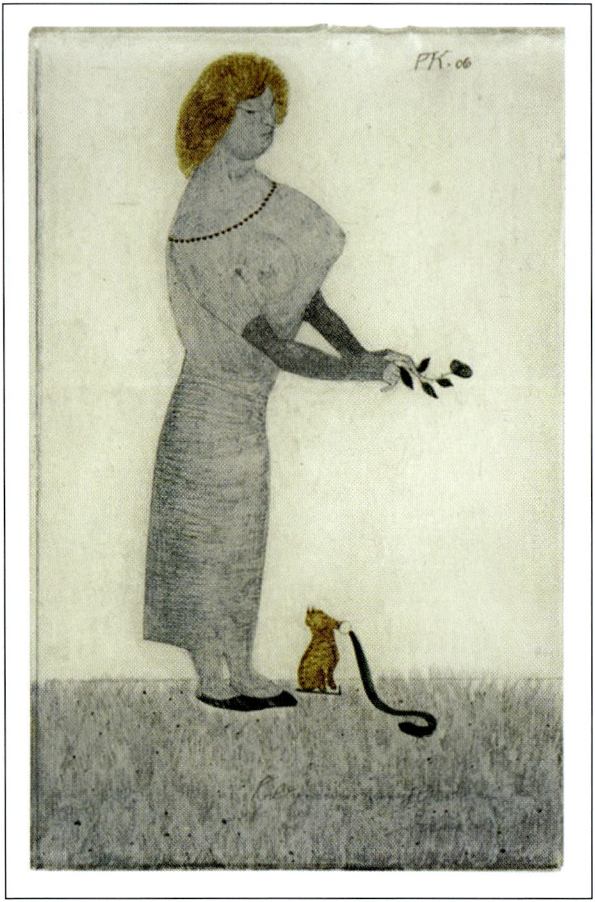

FLOWER BED

1913, Solomon R. Guggenheim Museum, New York City
28.2 × 33.7 cm, Oil on cardboard

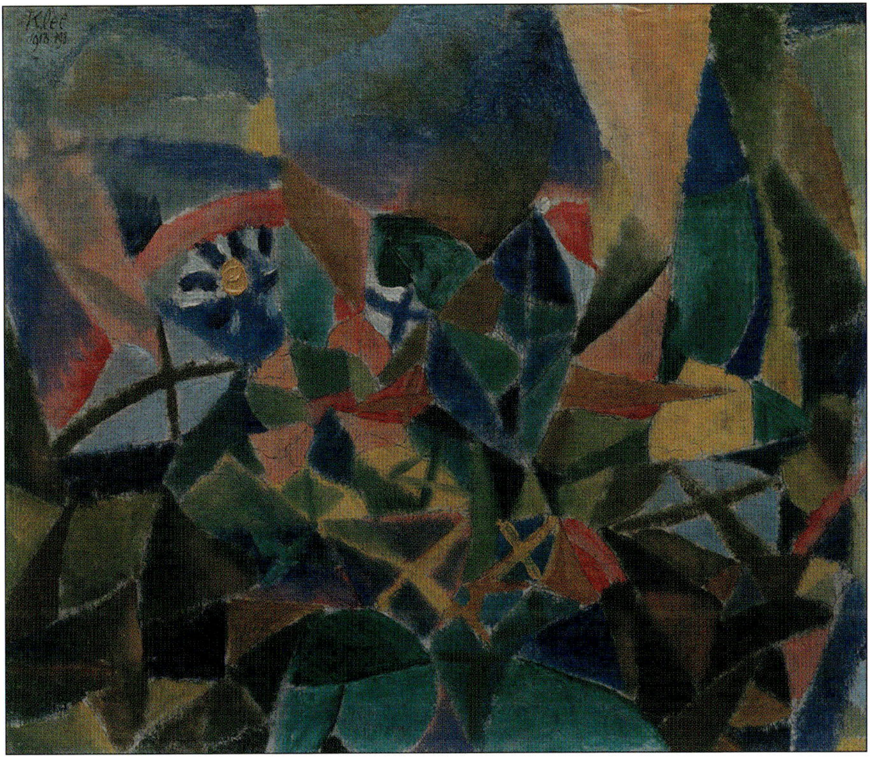

Plate 5

IN THE KAIROUAN STYLE, TRANSPOSED IN A MODERATE WAY

1914, Los Angeles County Museum of Art

14.5 x 21.5 cm, Watercolor and pencil on paper on bristol board

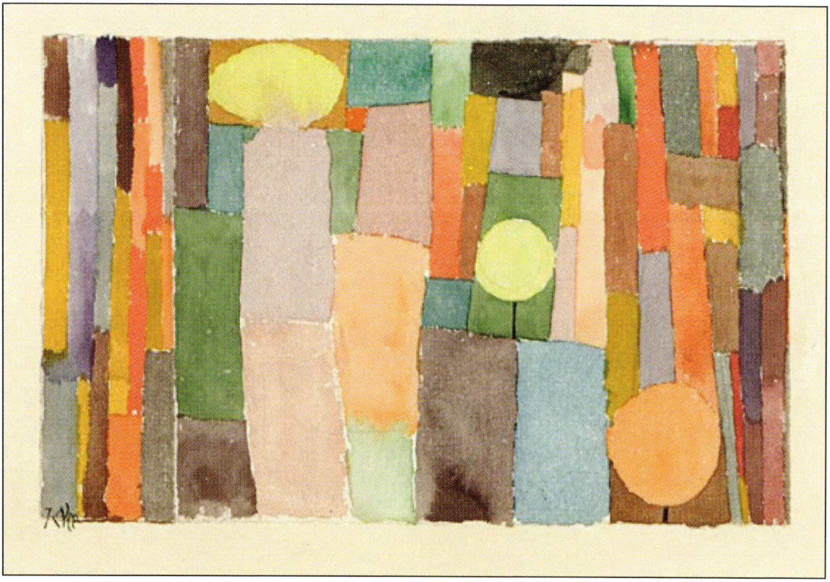

AFTER A SKETCH FROM ZURICH

1914, The Barnes Foundation, Philadelphia
11.4 x 13.3 cm, Watercolor with graphite underdrawing on wove paper; artist-mounted to paperboard

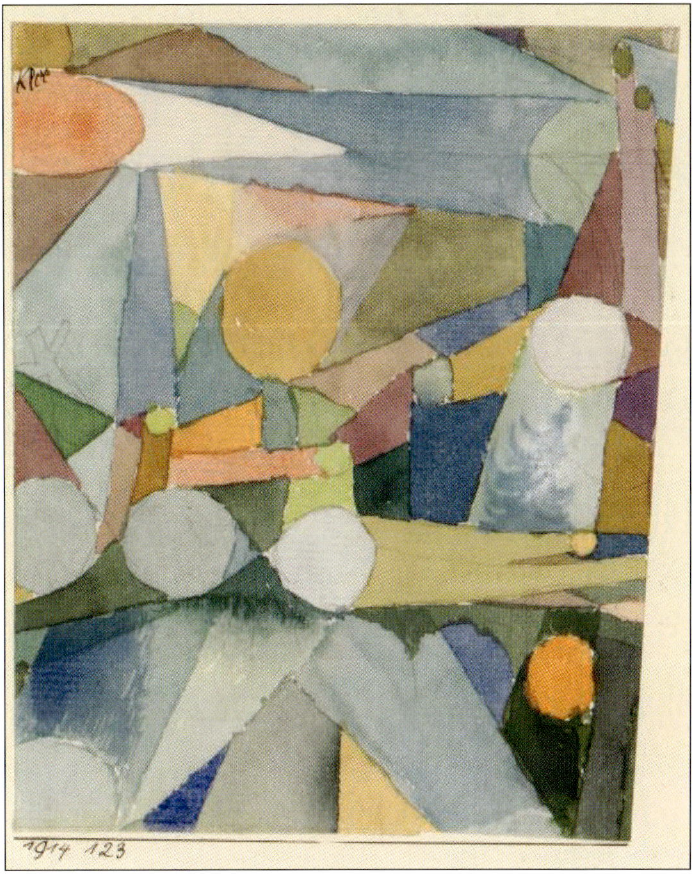

Plate 7

SOUTHERN GARDEN

1914, Kunstmuseum Basel, Switzerland

11.4 x 13.6 cm, Watercolor on paper, mounted on cardboard

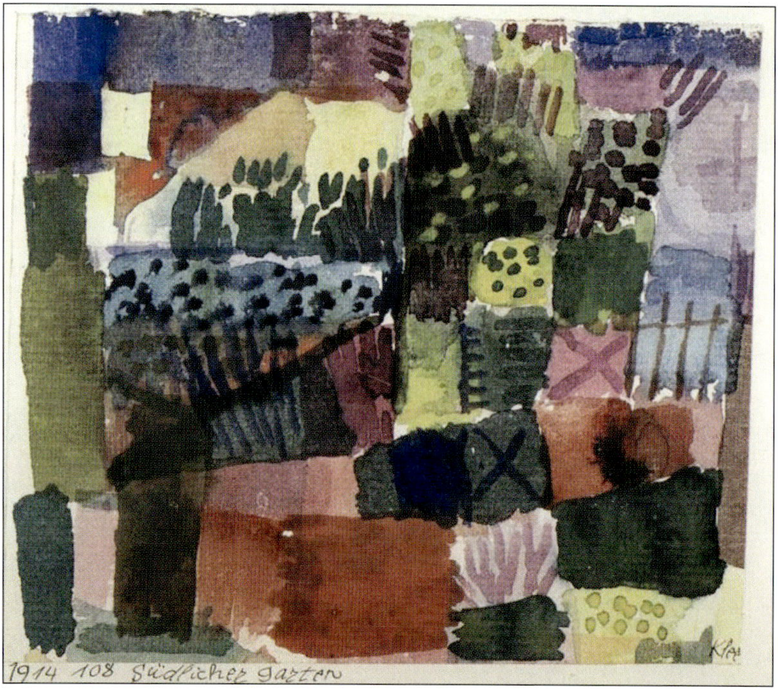

Plate 8

IN THE HOUSES OF ST. GERMAINE

1914, Zentrum Paul Klee, Bern, Switzerland

15.5 x 15.9 cm, Watercolor on paper on cardboard

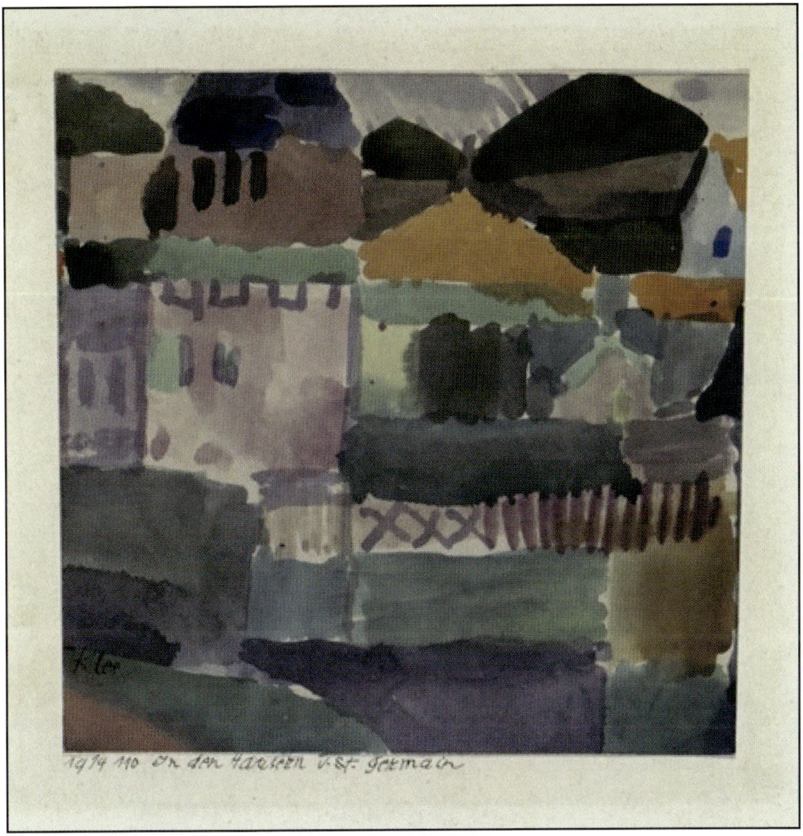

Plate 9

MOVEMENT OF VAULTED CHAMBERS

1915, The Metropolitan Museum of Art, New York City
20 x 25.2 cm, Watercolor on paper

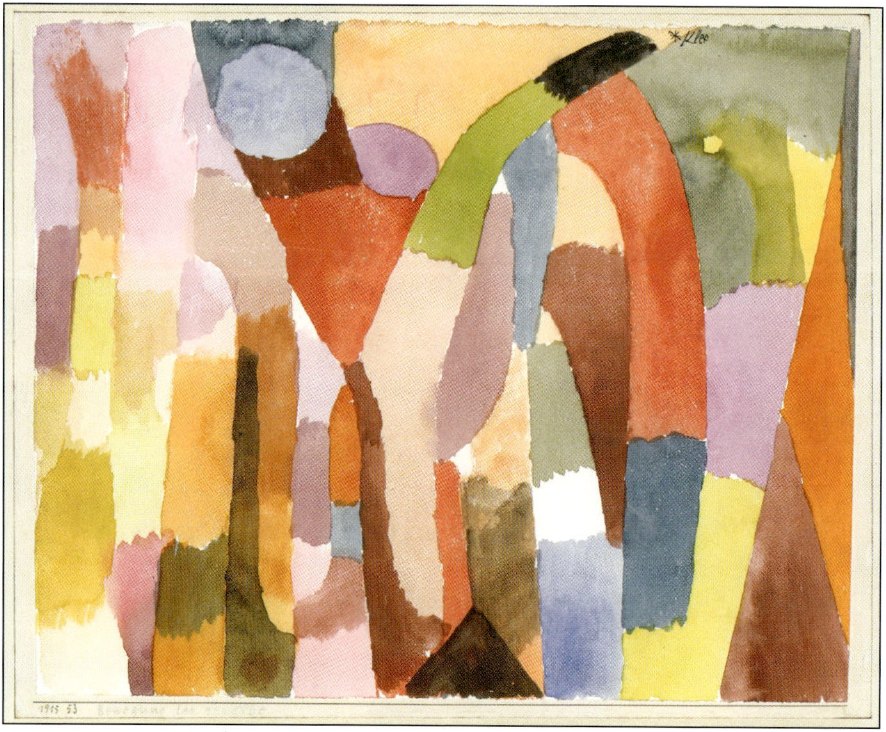

Plate 10

THE CHAPEL

1917, Beyeler Foundation, Riehen, Switzerland
29.5 x 15 cm, Watercolor and white tempera on paper on cardboard

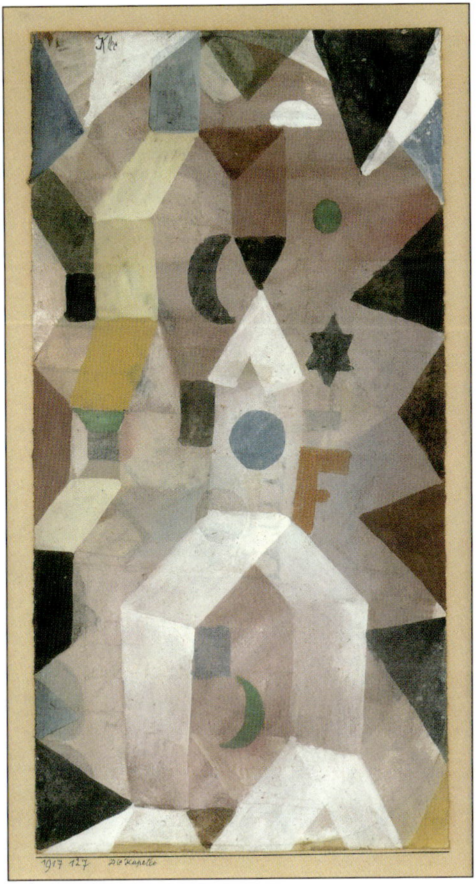

CASTLE GARDEN

1919, Kunstmuseum Basel, Switzerland
29.5 x 21 cm, Watercolor on chalk primer on paper, mounted on silver paper, mounted on cardboard

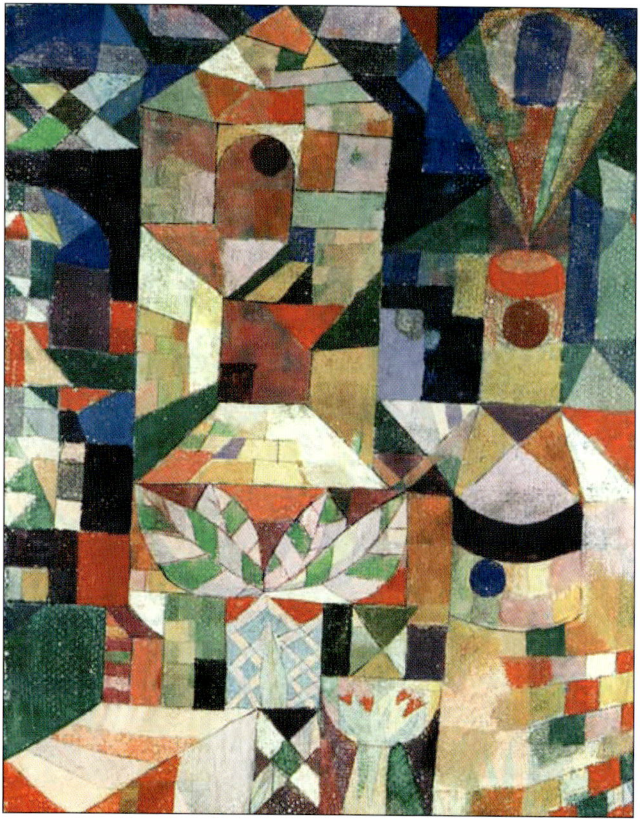

SCHOOLHOUSE

1920, The Art Institute of Chicago
36.8 x 31.8 cm, Oil on paper, on board

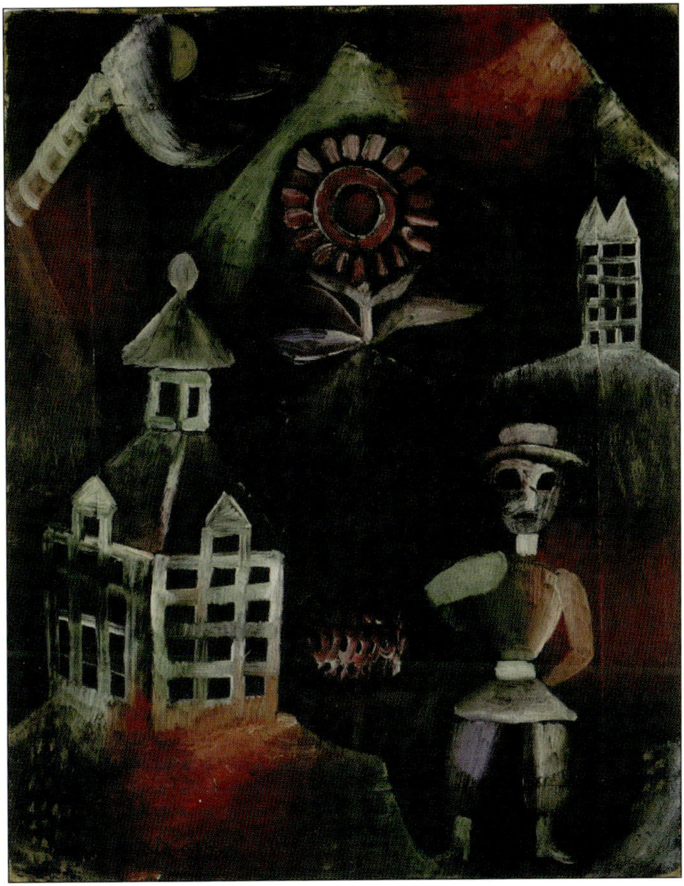

Plate 13

THEY'RE BITING

1920, Tate Modern, London

31.1 x 23.5 cm, Watercolor and oil paint on paper

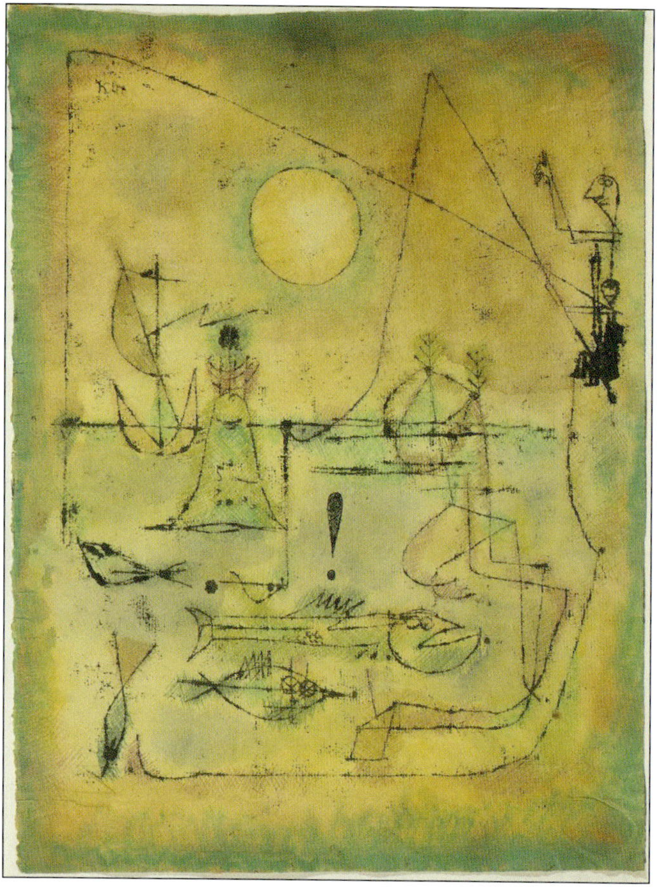

ROSE GARDEN

1920, Lenbachhauss, Munich, Germany
49 x 42.5 cm, Oil on cardboard

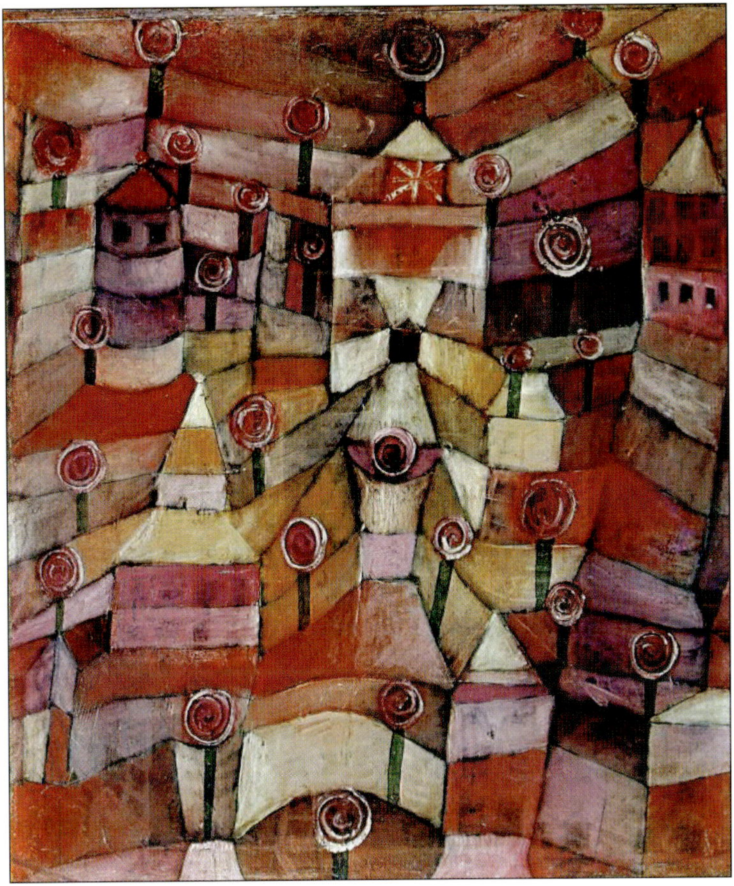

Plate 15

MIRACULOUS LANDING

1920, The Metropolitan Museum of Art, New York City
23.6 x 31.8 cm, Watercolor, transferred printing ink, and ink on paper

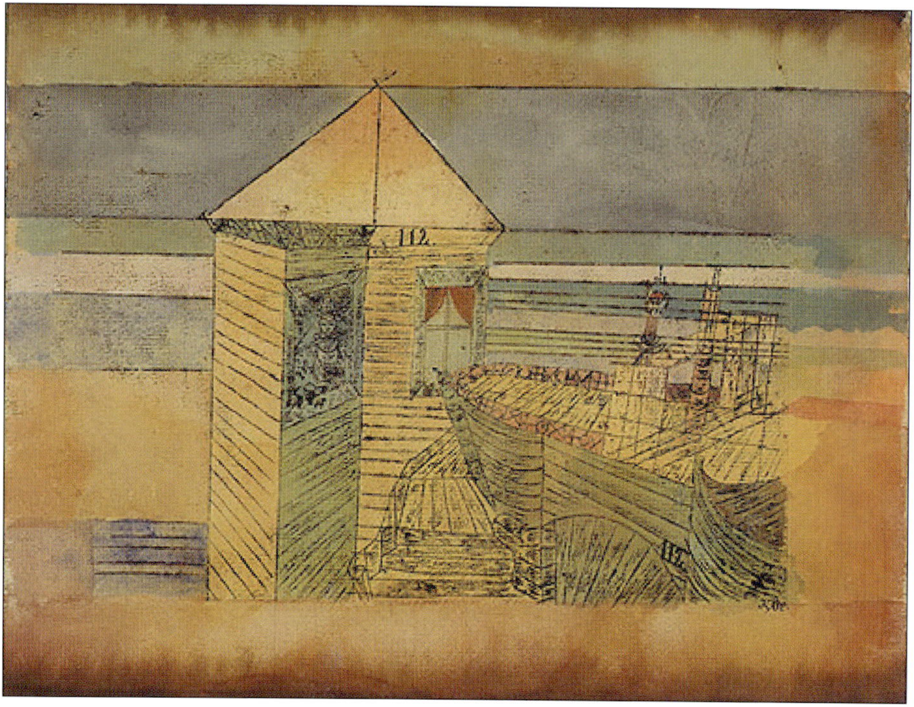

BAD BAND

1920, The Barnes Foundation, Philadelphia
24 x 15.2 cm, Watercolor, pen and ink, and black crayon (?) on thin paper; artist-mounted to paperboard

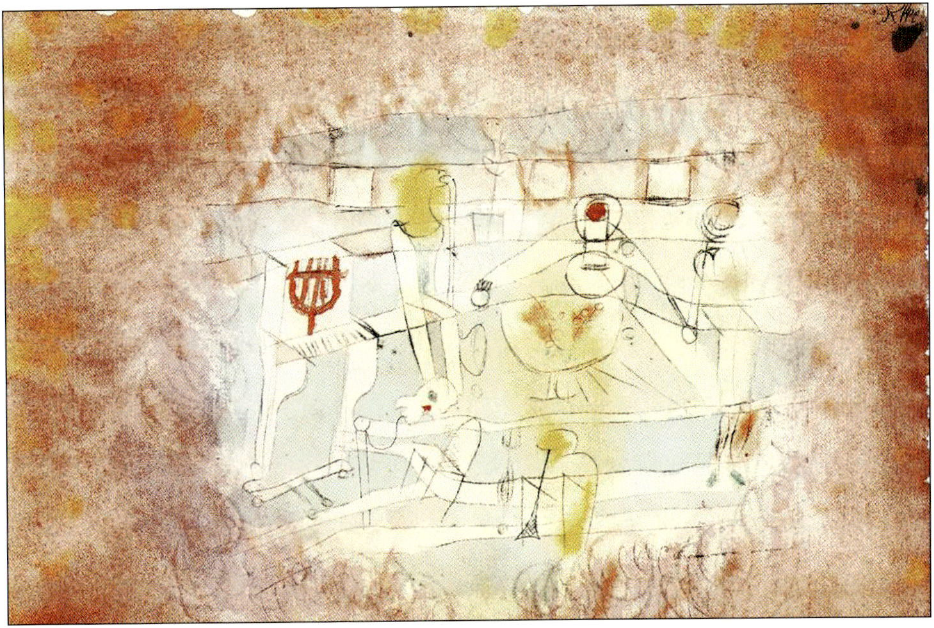

Plate 17

HOFFMANNESQUE FAIRY TALE SCENE

1921, San Francisco Museum of Modern Art

31.59 x 23.02 cm, Lithograph

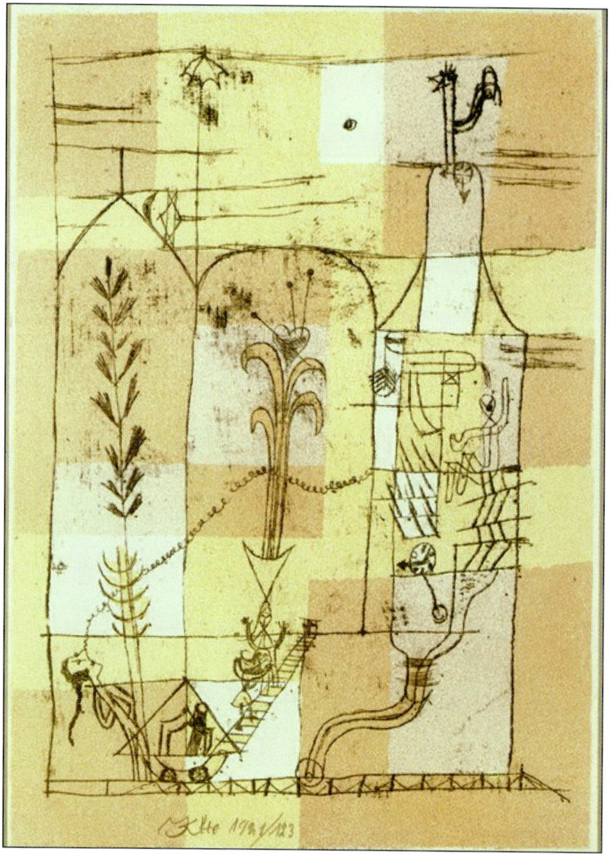

ROOM PERSPECTIVE WITH INHABITANTS

1921, Zentrum Paul Klee, Bern, Switzerland

48.5 x 31.7 cm, Oil transfer drawing and watercolor on paper on cardboard

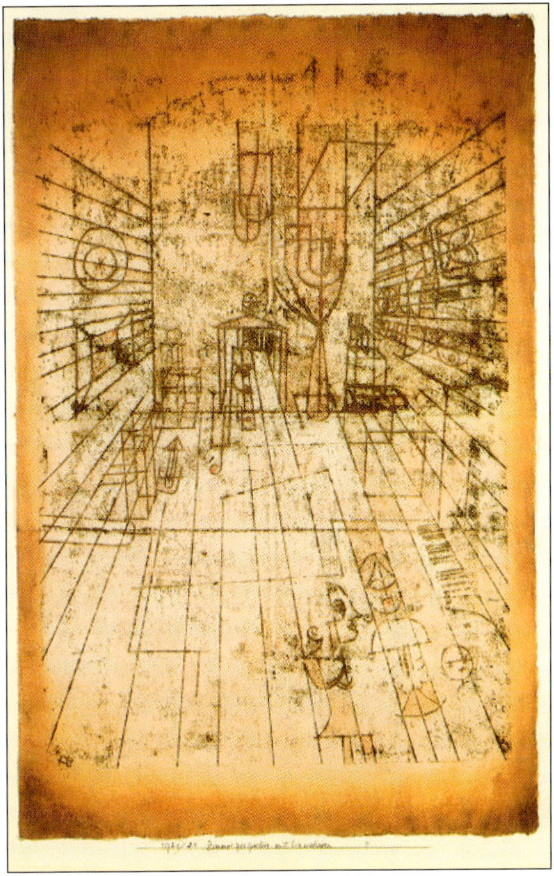

Plate 19

TROPICAL TWILIGHT

1921, Beyeler Foundation, Riehen, Switzerland

33.5 x 23 cm, Oil on white primer on paper on cardboard

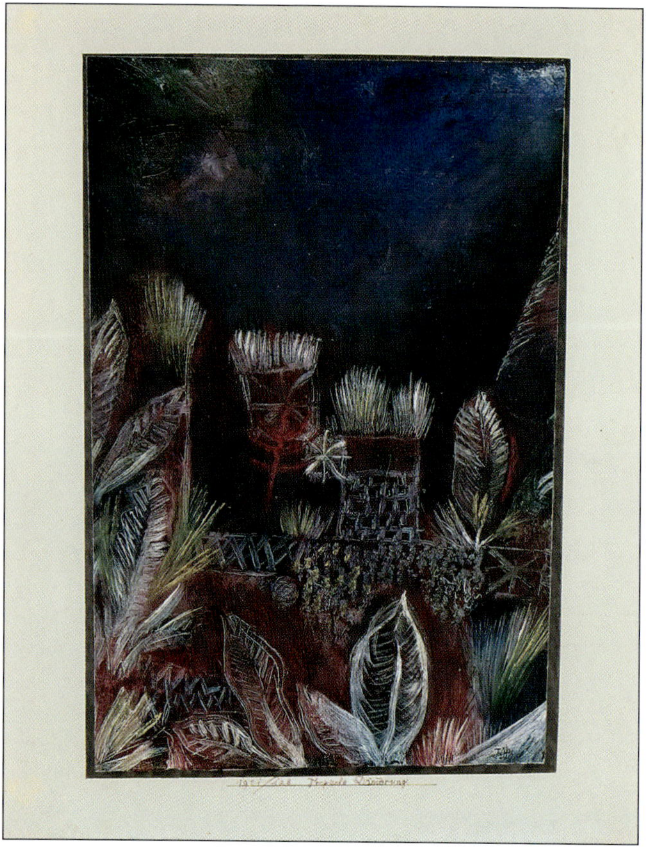

COMEDY

1921, Tate Modern, London

30.5 x 45.4 cm, Watercolor and oil paint on paper

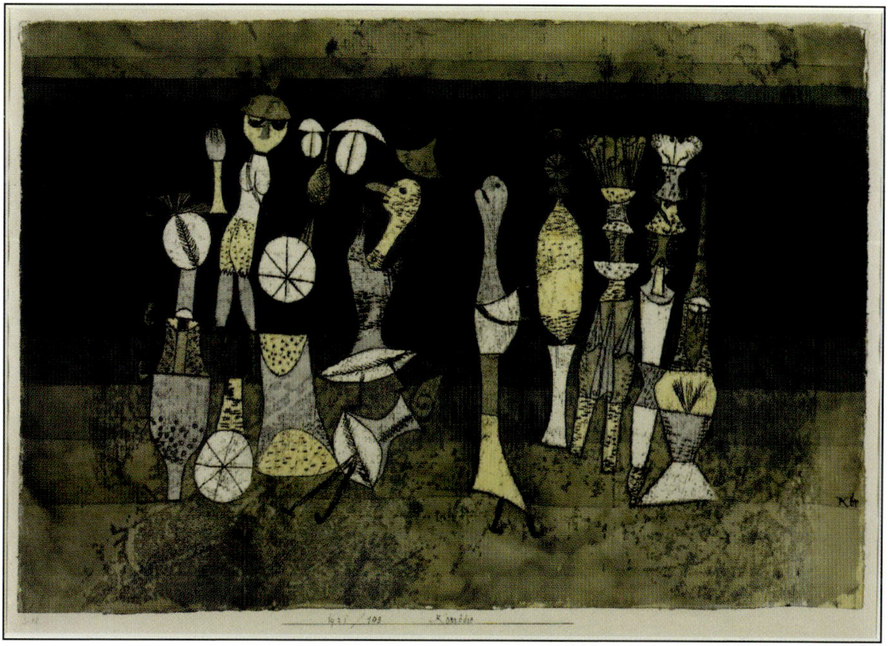

Plate 21

TALE À LA HOFFMANN

1921, The Metropolitan Museum of Art, New York City
31.1 x 24.1 cm, Watercolor, graphite, and transferred printing ink on paper bordered with metallic foil, mounted on cardboard

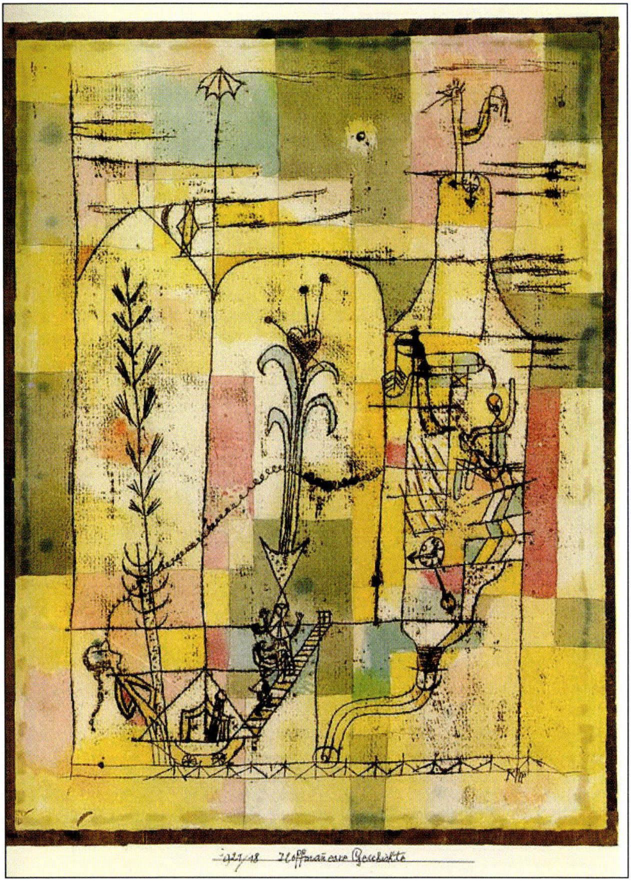

ADAM AND LITTLE EVE

1921, The Metropolitan Museum of Art, New York City

31.4 x 21.9 cm, Watercolor and transferred printing ink on paper mounted on cardboard

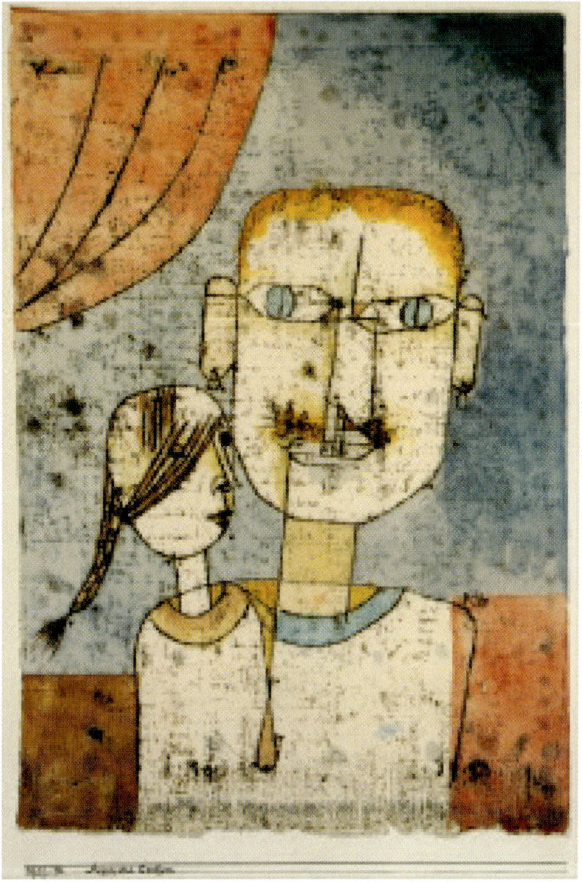

Plate 23

TWITTERING MACHINE

1922, Museum of Modern Art, New York City

64.1 x 48.3 cm, Oil transfer drawing, watercolor and ink on paper with gouache and ink borders, on board

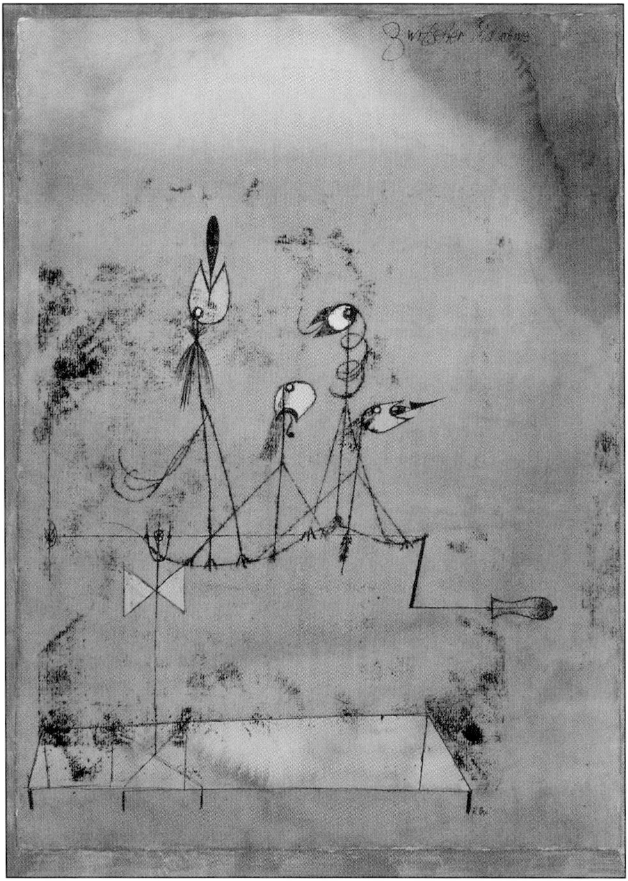

GROWTH OF THE NIGHT PLANTS

1922, Pinakothek der Moderne, Munich, Germany

33.9 x 47.2 cm, Oil on cardboard

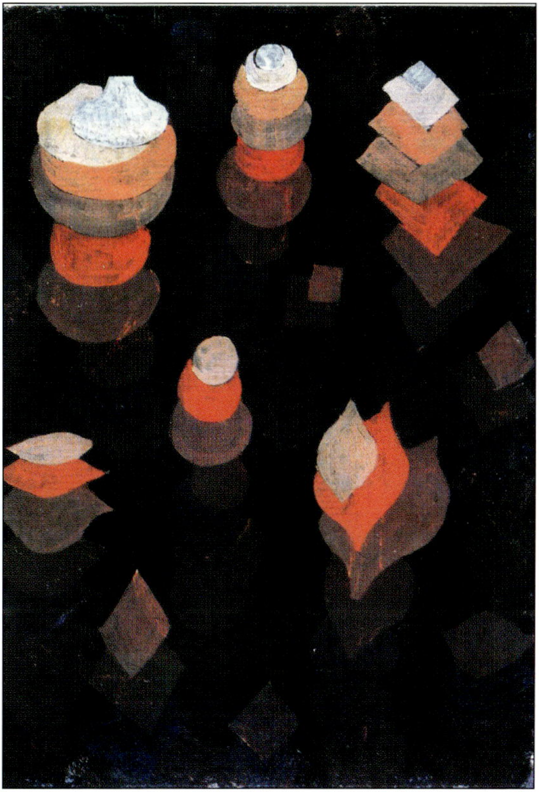

Plate 25

SEPARATION IN THE EVENING

1922, Zentrum Paul Klee, Bern, Switzerland

33.5 x 23.2 cm, Watercolor and pencil on paper on cardboard

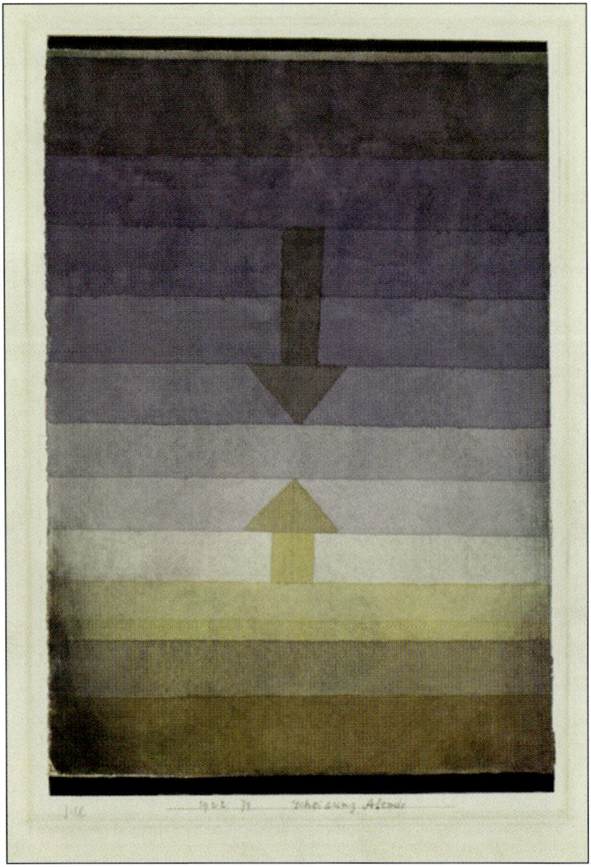

RED BALLOON

1922, Solomon R. Guggenheim Museum, New York City

31.7 x 31.1 cm, Oil (and oil transfer drawing?) on chalk-primed gauze, mounted on board

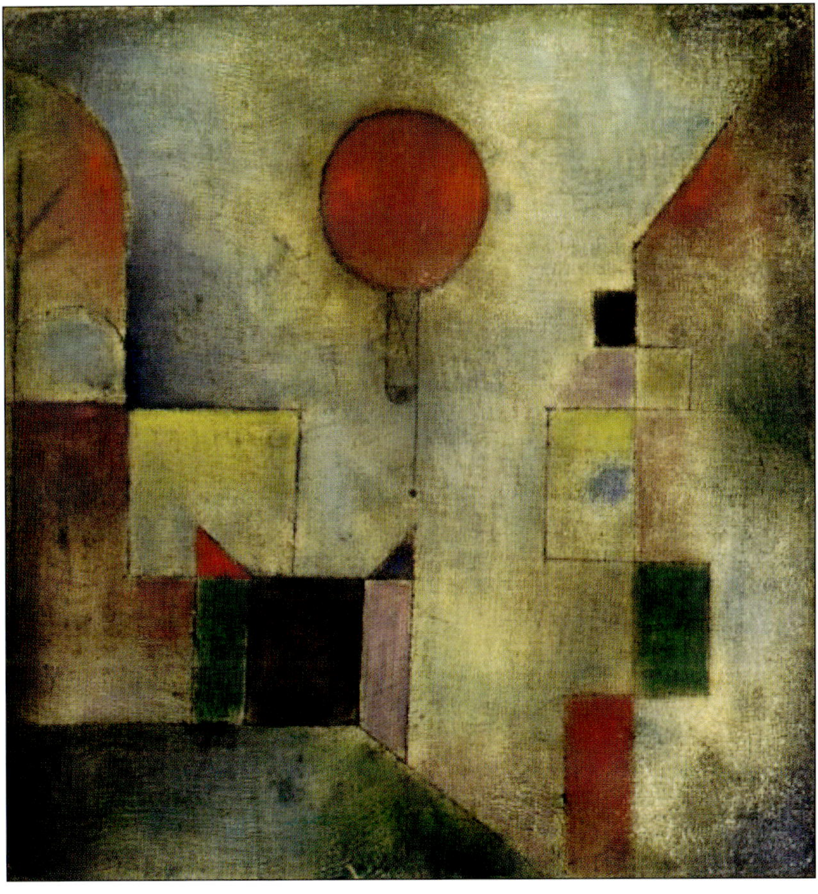

Plate 27

A YOUNG LADY'S ADVENTURE

1922, Tate Modern, London
62.5 x 48 cm, Watercolor on paper

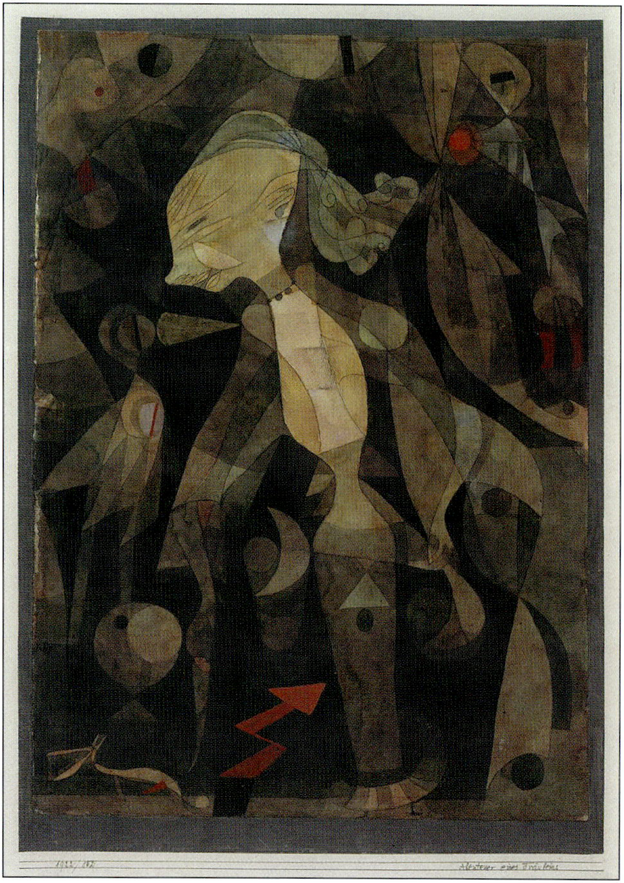

SENECIO (SOON TO BE AGED)

1922, Kunstmuseum Basel, Switzerland
40.3 x 37.4 cm, Oil on chalk primer on gauze on cardboard

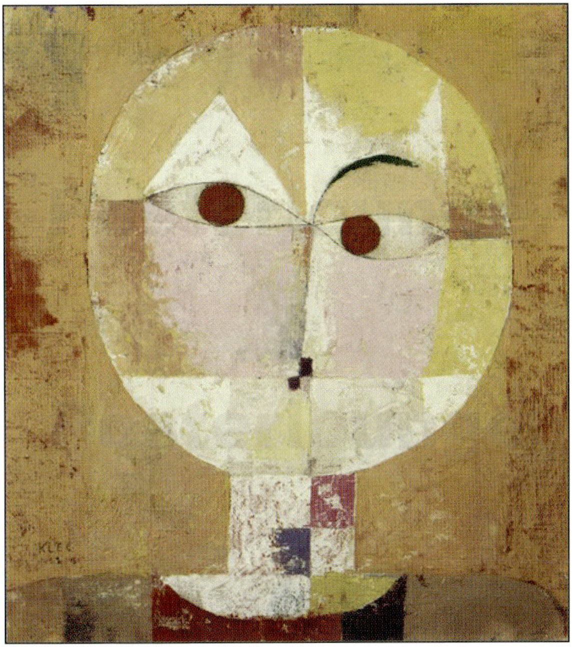

Plate 29

BEFORE THE LIGHTNING

1923, Beyeler Foundation, Riehen, Switzerland
28 x 31.5 cm, Watercolor and pencil on paper, top and bottom edges with gouache, watercolor, and quill on cardboard

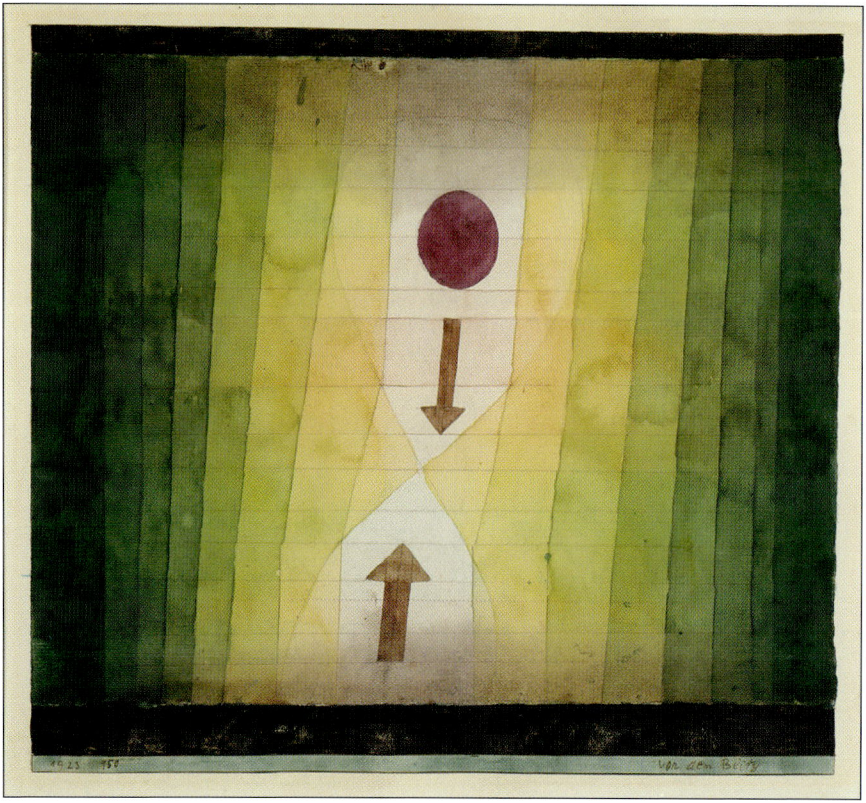

SEVENTEEN, INSANE

1923, Kunstmuseum Basel, Switzerland

22.3 x 28.6 cm, Pen and watercolor on paper, mounted on cardboard

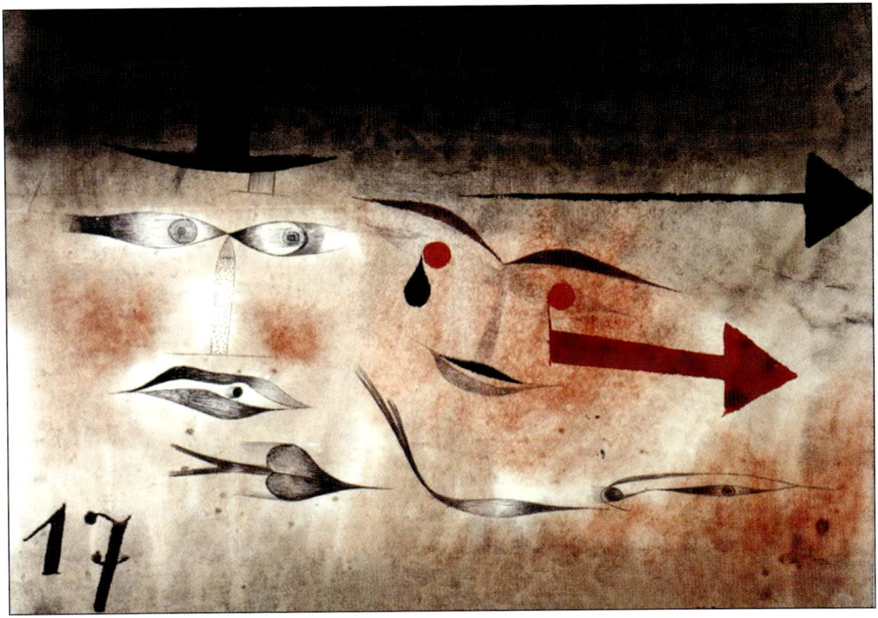

Plate 31

THE SUBLIME ASPECT (POSTCARD FOR THE BAUHAUS EXHIBITION)

1923, The Art Institute of Chicago

14.4 x 7.3 cm (image); 15.1 x 10.6 cm (sheet), Lithograph in black with additions of blue, red, and yellow on cream postcard paper

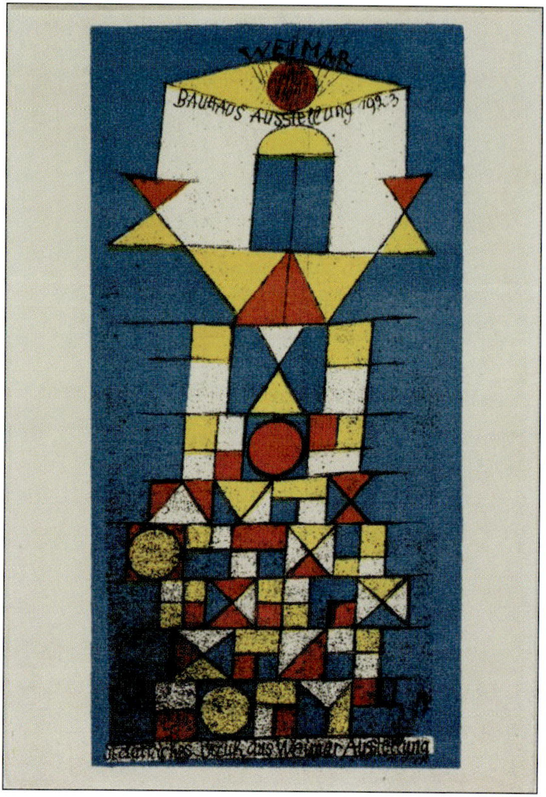

BATTLE SCENE FROM THE COMIC FANTASTIC OPERA "THE SEAFARER"

1923, Kunstmuseum Basel, Switzerland
34.5 x 50 cm, Oil, pencil, watercolor, and gouache on paper; framed and mounted on cardboard

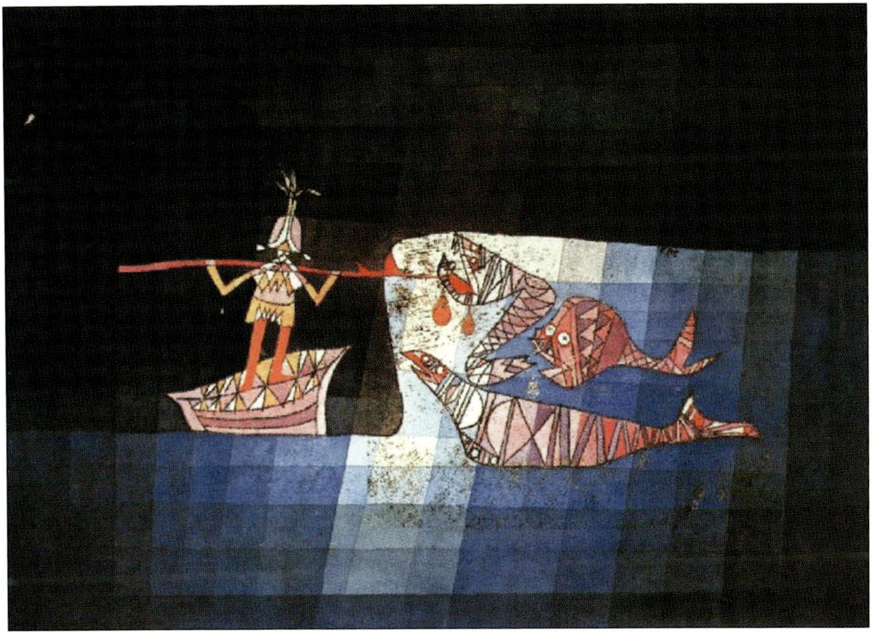

GARDEN ON DEBRIS

1923-24, The Art Institute of Chicago
26.8 x 25.4 cm, Watercolor and black ink transfer on cream wove paper, mounted on cream card

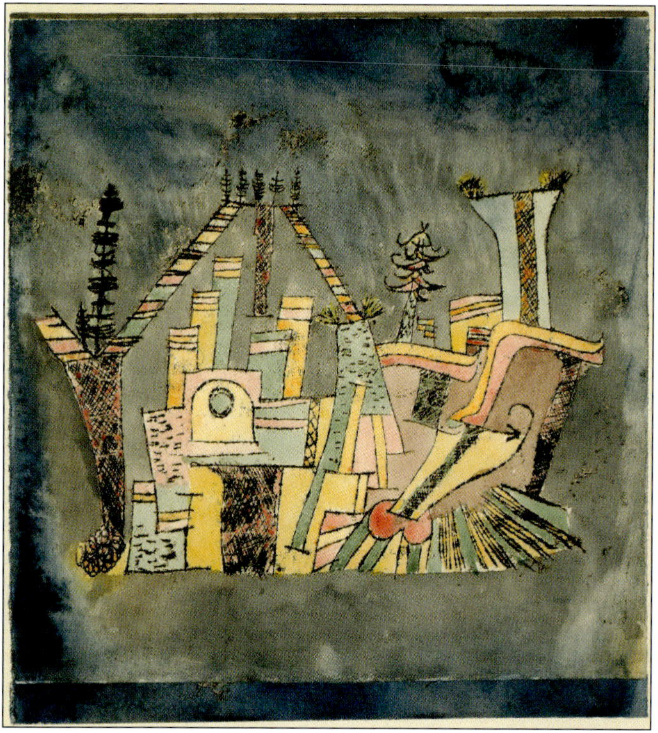

GIRL POSSESSED

1924, Beyeler Foundation, Riehen, Switzerland
44.2 x 29.2 cm, Oil transfer drawing and watercolor on paper on cardboard

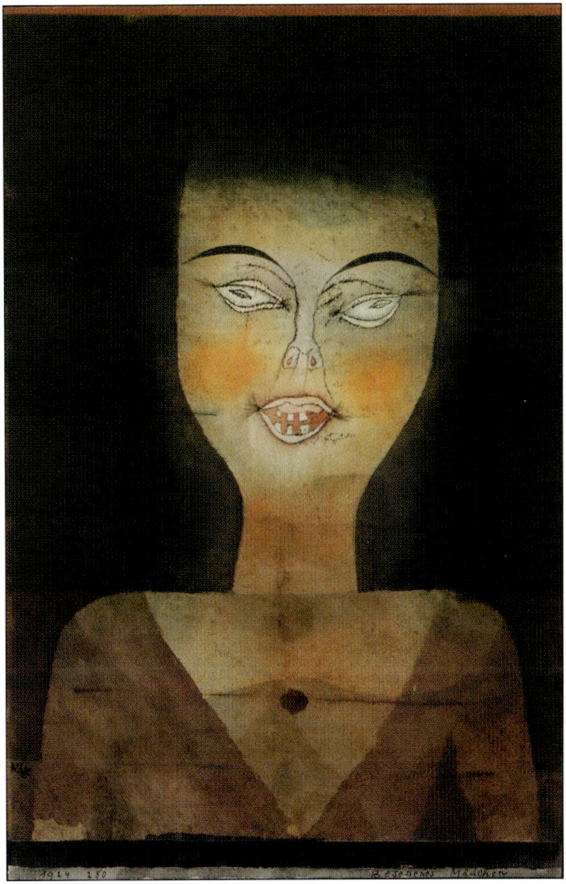

ACTOR'S MASK

1924, Museum of Modern Art, New York City
36.7 x 33.8 cm, Oil on canvas mounted on board

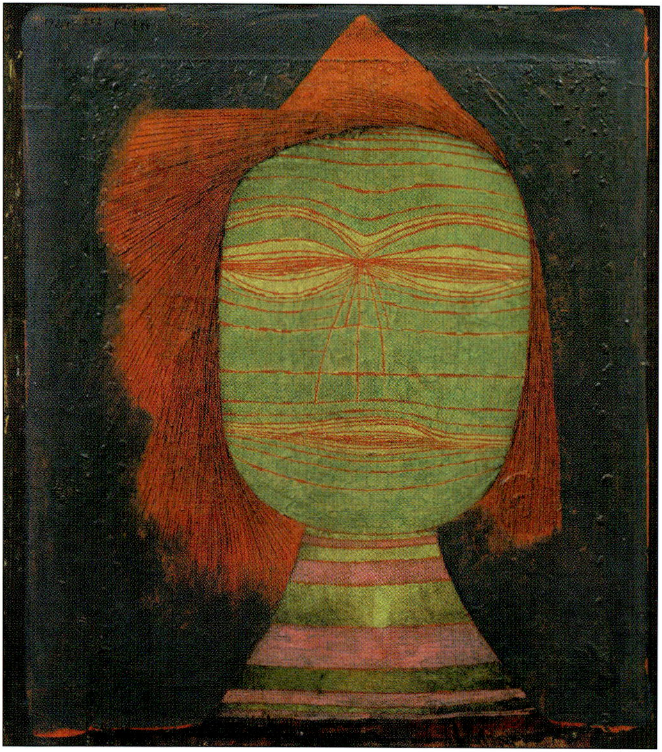

FISH PICTURE

1925, Museum Sammlung Rosengart, Lucerne, Switzerland
64 x 43 cm, Oil transfer drawing, pen and ink, and watercolor on plaster priming on gauze, on blue, primed cardboard; original painted frame strips

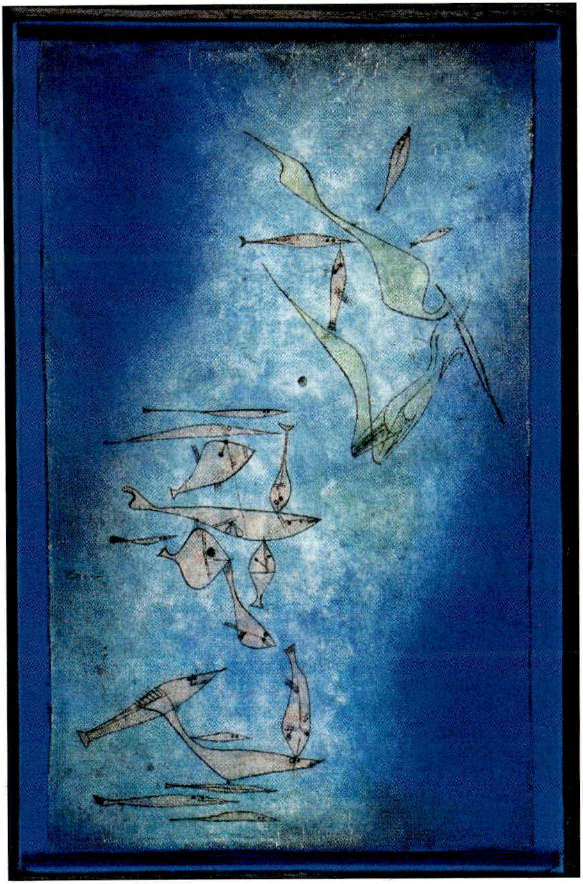

Plate 37

FISH MAGIC

1925, Philadelphia Museum of Art
77.1 x 98.4 cm, Oil and watercolor on canvas on panel

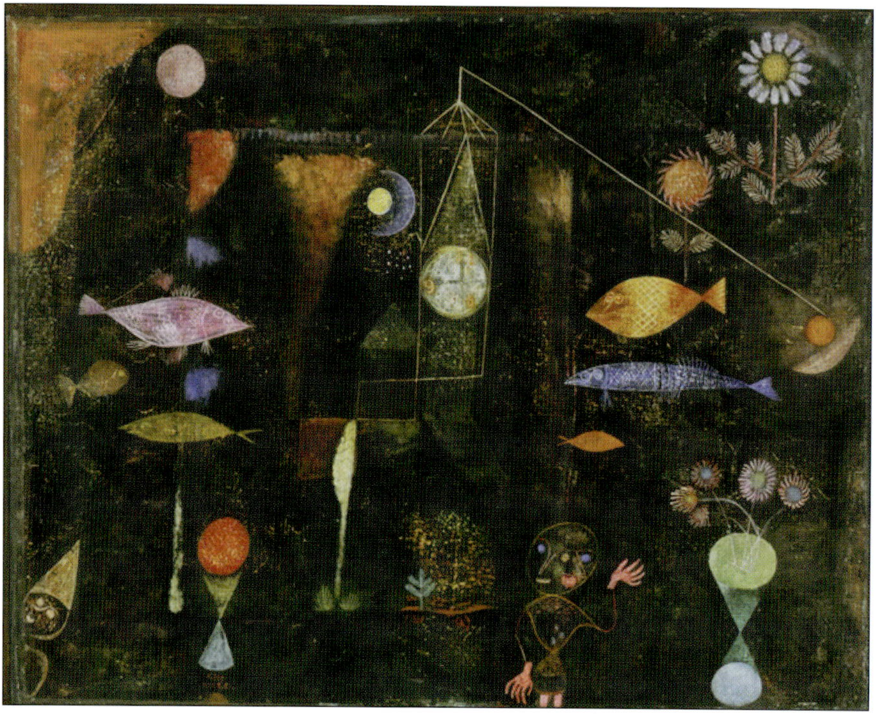

ALTER KLANG

1925, Kunstmuseum Basel, Switzerland
38.3 x 38 cm, Oil on cardboard

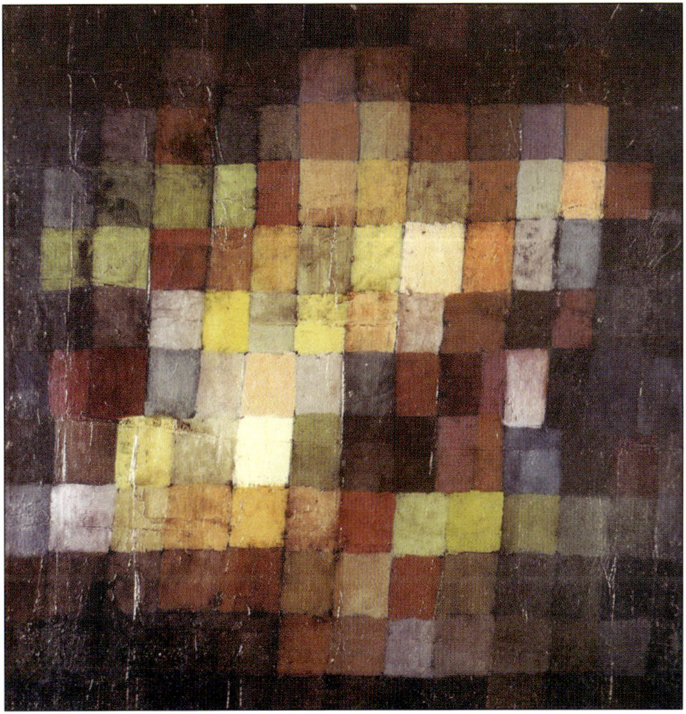

Plate 39

PLACE SIGNS

1926, The Barnes Foundation, Philadelphia

25.5 x 36.7 cm, Watercolor on handmade wove paper; artist-mounted to paperboard

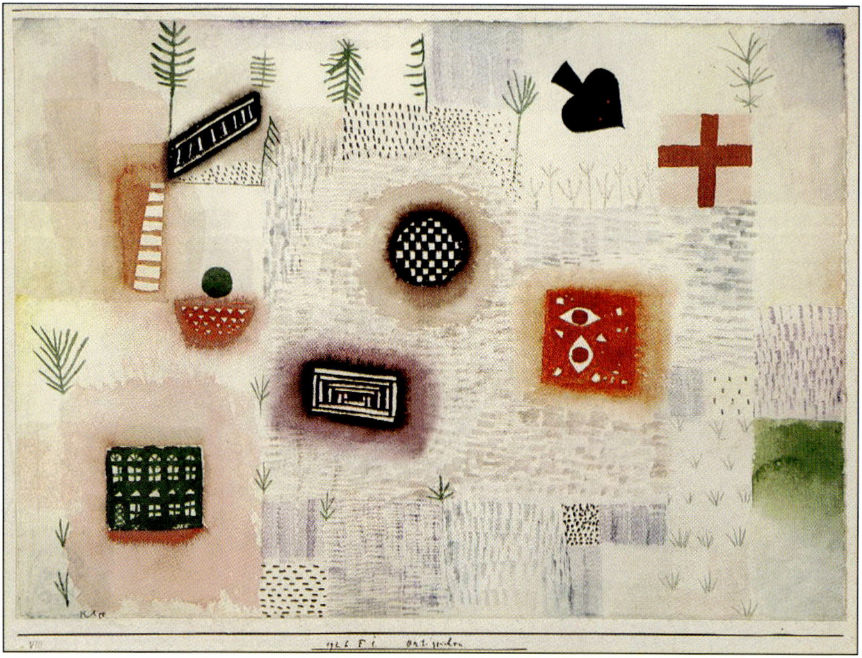

AROUND THE FISH

1926, Museum of Modern Art, New York City
46.7 x 63.8 cm, Oil and tempera on canvas mounted on cardboard

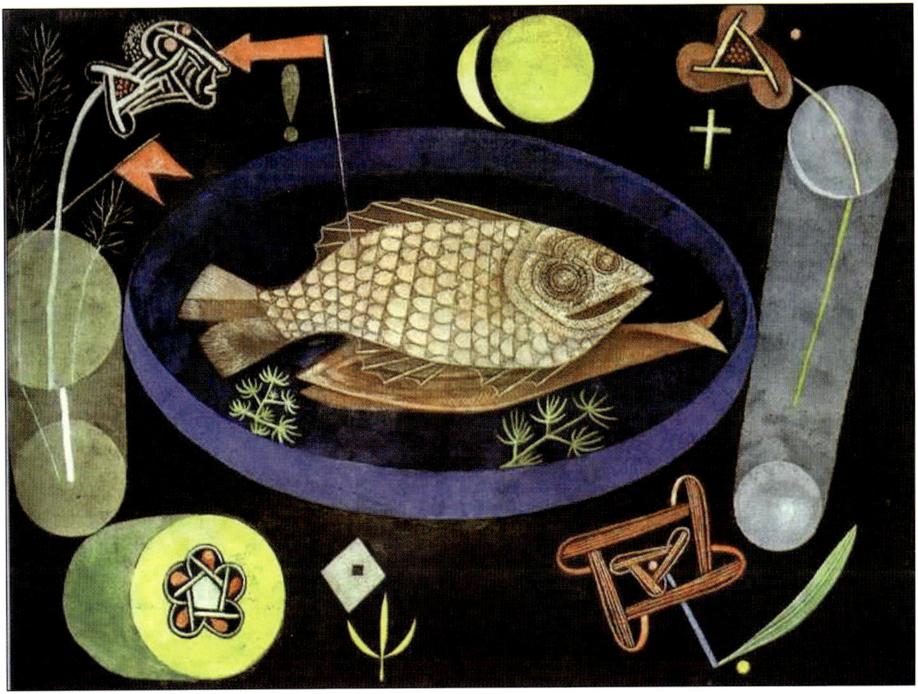

Plate 41

HISTORICAL SITE

1927, Tate Modern, London

35.5 x 48.7 cm, Watercolor and ink on paper on board

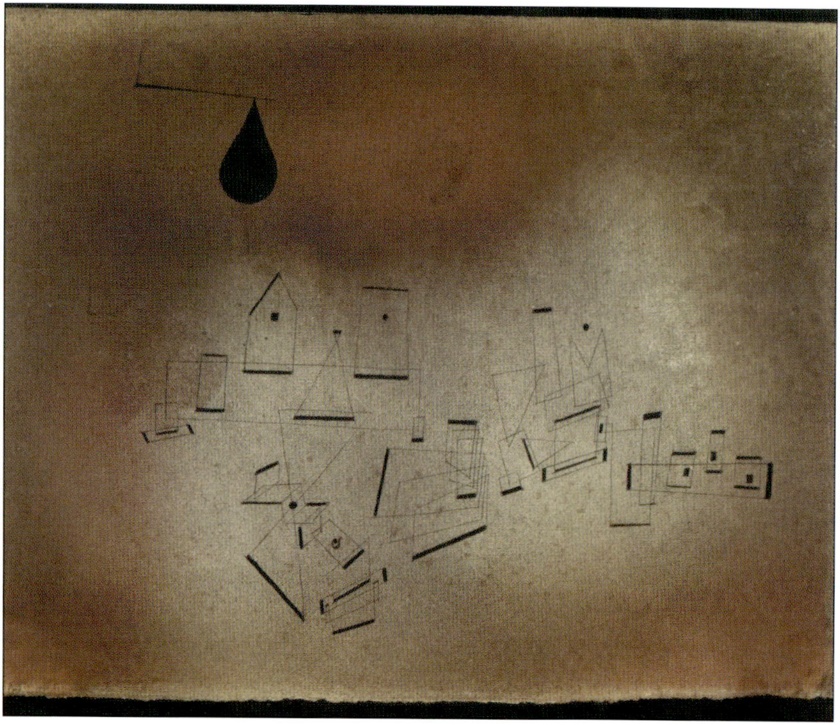

SEASIDE RESORT IN THE SOUTH OF FRANCE

1927, Tate Modern, London

32.7 x 48.8 cm, Graphite, crayon and watercolor on paper on board

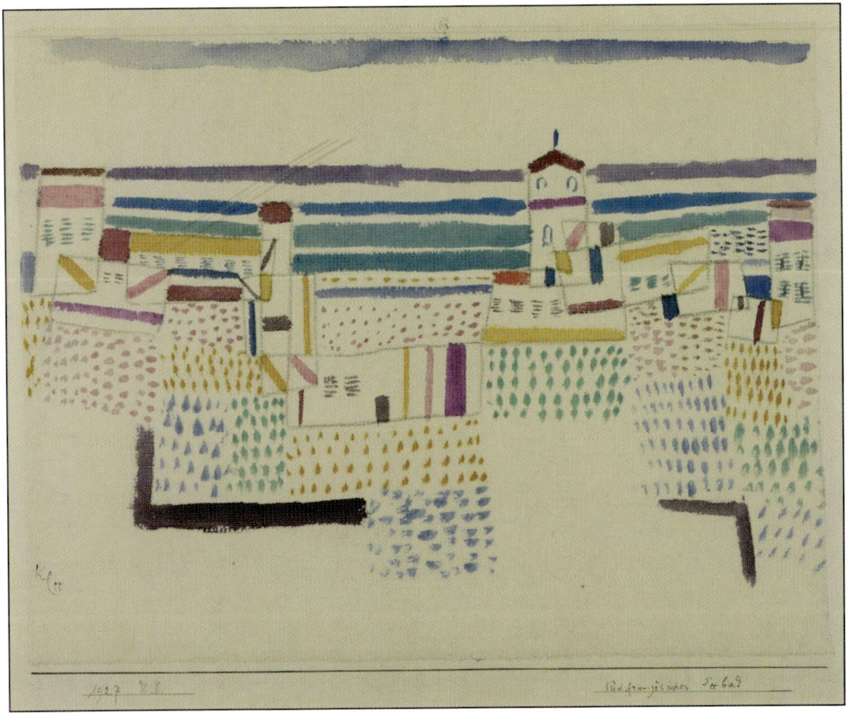

Plate 43

PASTORALE (RHYTHMS)

1927, Museum of Modern Art, New York City
69.3 x 52.4 cm, Tempera on canvas mounted on wood

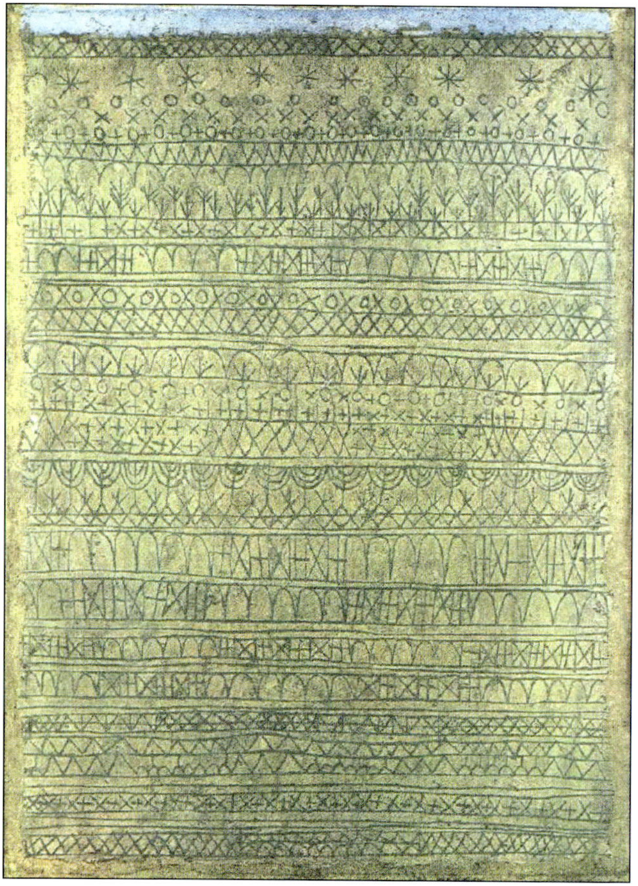

CAT AND BIRD

1928, Musuem of Modern Art, New York City
38.1 x 53.2 cm, Oil and ink on gessoed canvas, mounted on wood

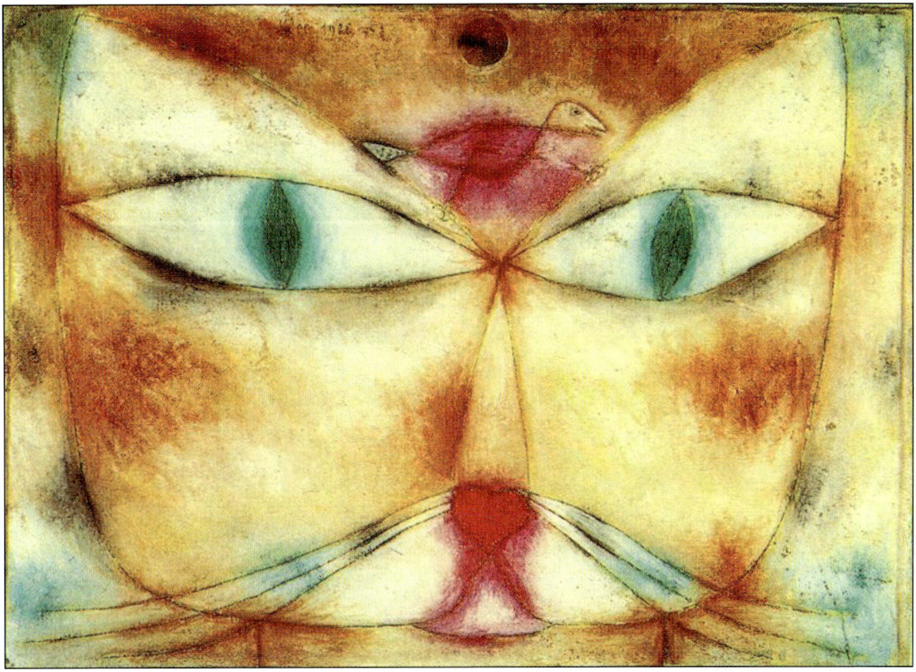

Plate 45

HIGHWAY AND BYWAYS

1929, Ludwig Museum, Cologne, Germany
83.7 x 67.5 cm, Oil on canvas

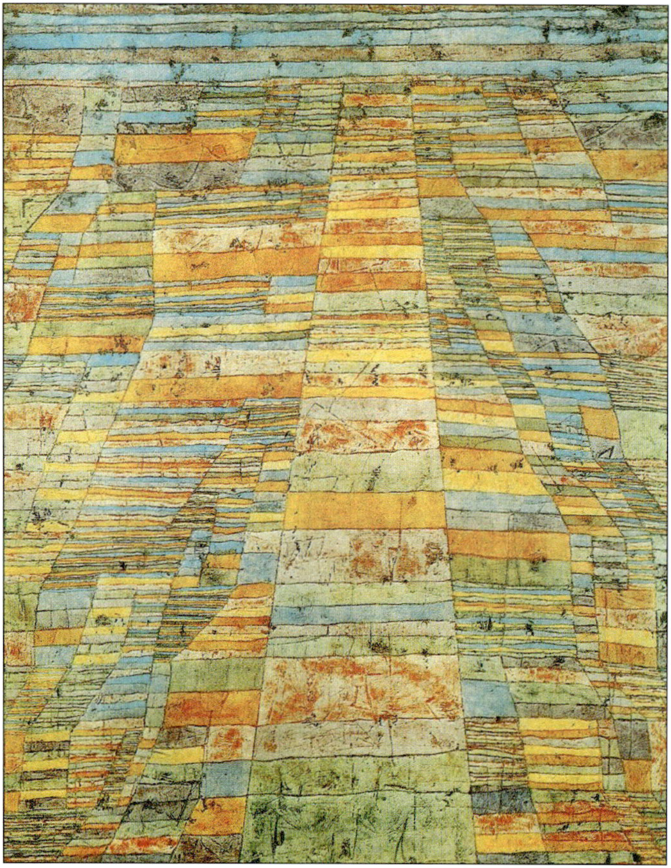

GARTENHAUS (SUMMER HOUSE)

1929, Albertina, Vienna, Austria

21 x 42 cm, Oil and watercolor on canvas on cardboard

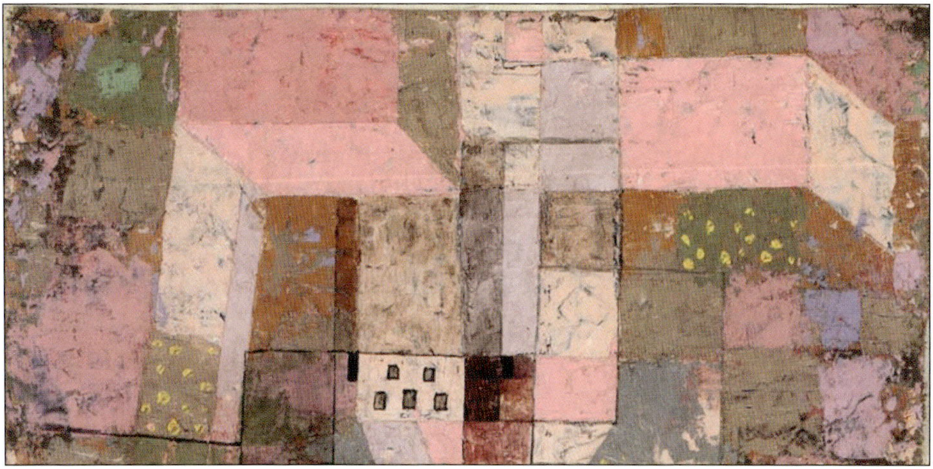

Plate 47

IN THE CURRENT SIX THRESHOLDS

1929, Solomon R. Guggenheim Museum, New York City
43.5 x 43.5 cm, Oil and tempera on canvas

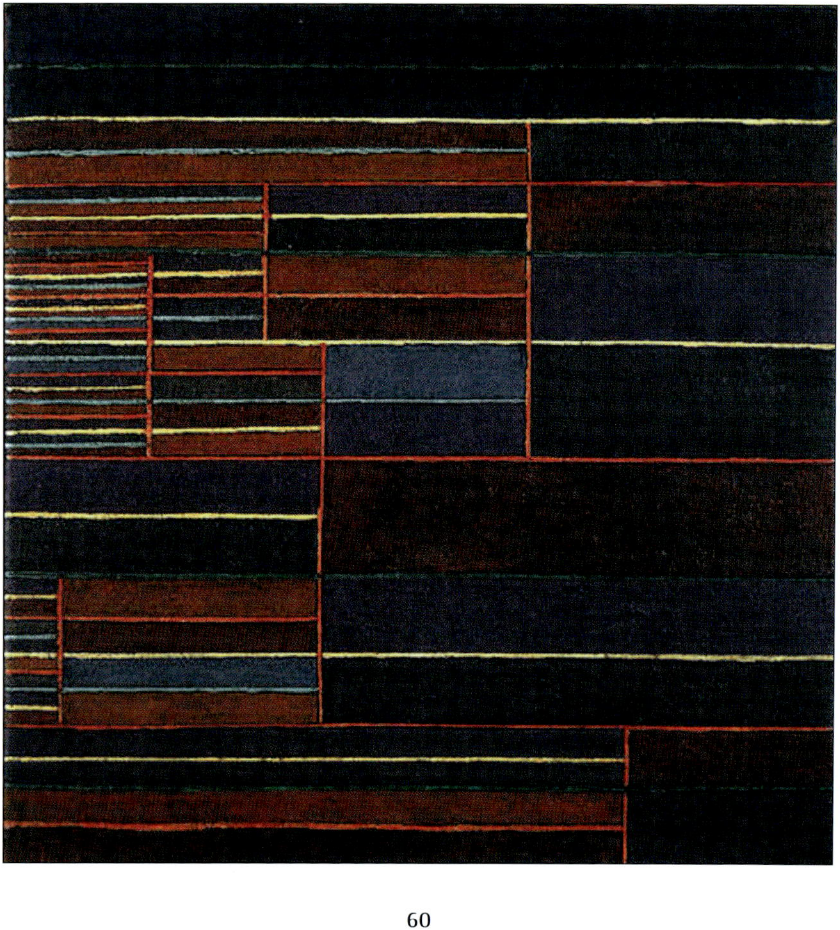

BURDENED CHILDREN

1930, Tate Modern, London

65 x 45.8 cm, Graphite, crayon and ink on paper on board

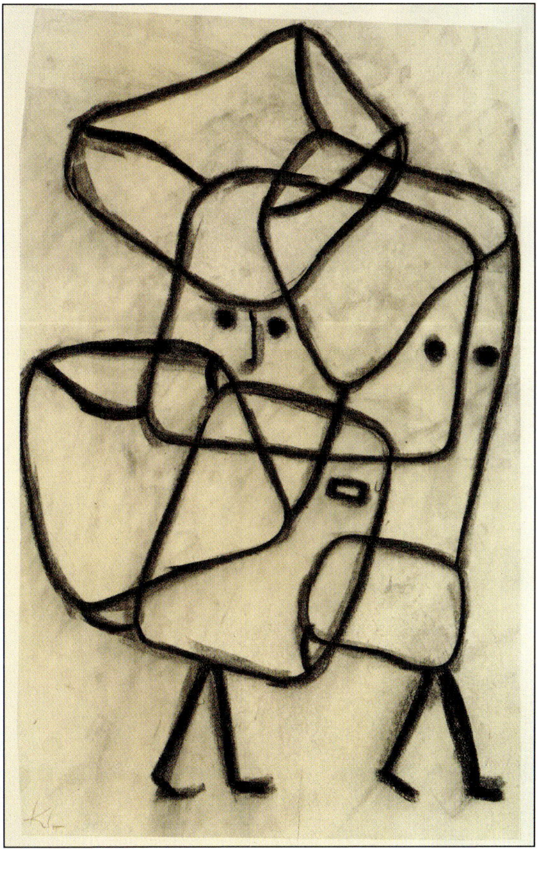

Plate 49

AD MARGINEM

1930, Kunstmuseum Basel, Switzerland
43.5 x 33 cm, Watercolor and pen on cardboard

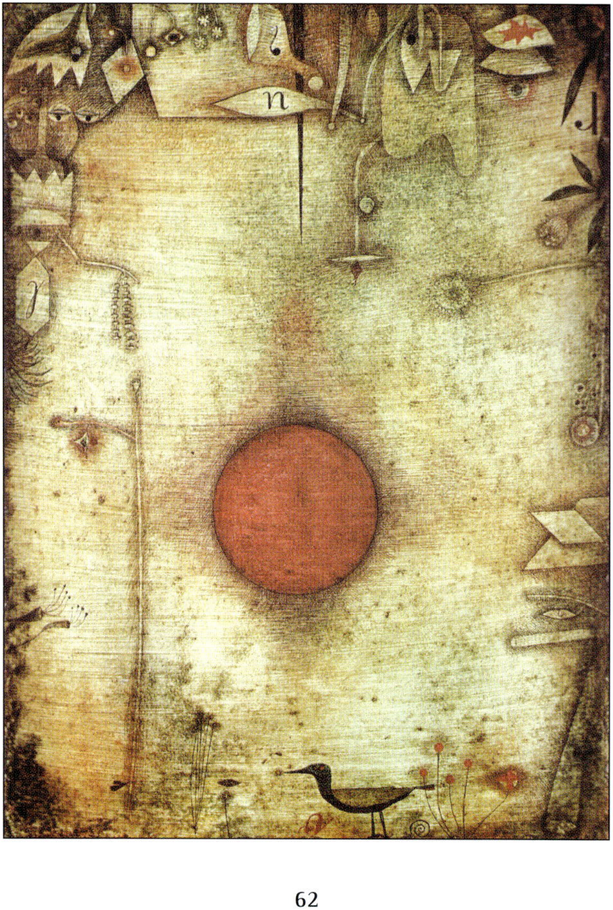

DIANA

1931, Beyeler Foundation, Riehen, Switzerland
80 x 60 cm, Oil on canvas

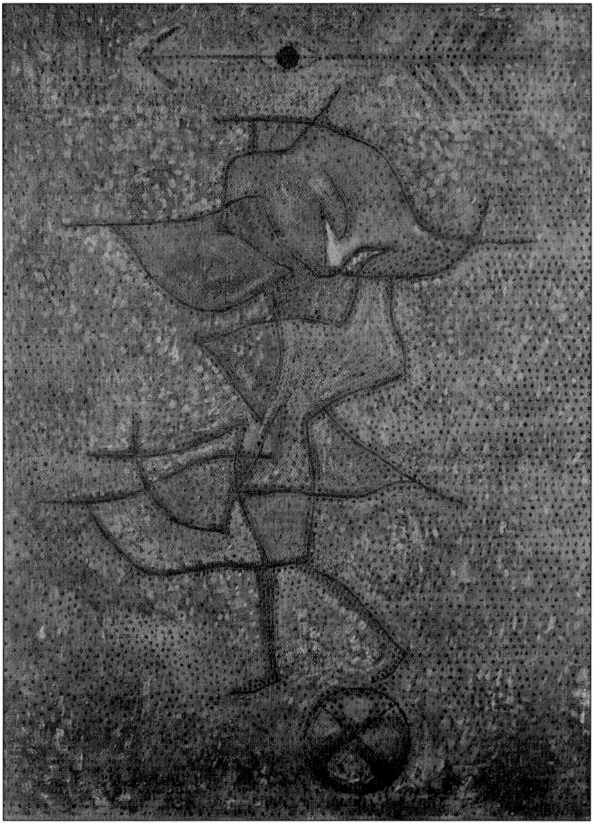

Plate 51

RISING STAR

1931, Beyeler Foundation, Riehen, Switzerland
63 x 50 cm, Oil on canvas

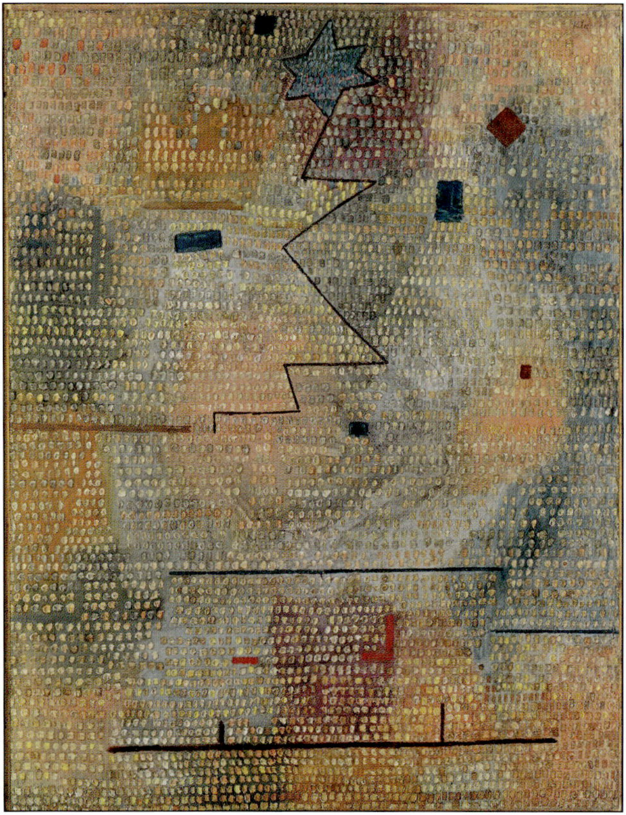

CASTLE GARDEN

1931, Museum of Modern Art, New York City
67.2 x 54.9 cm, Oil on canvas

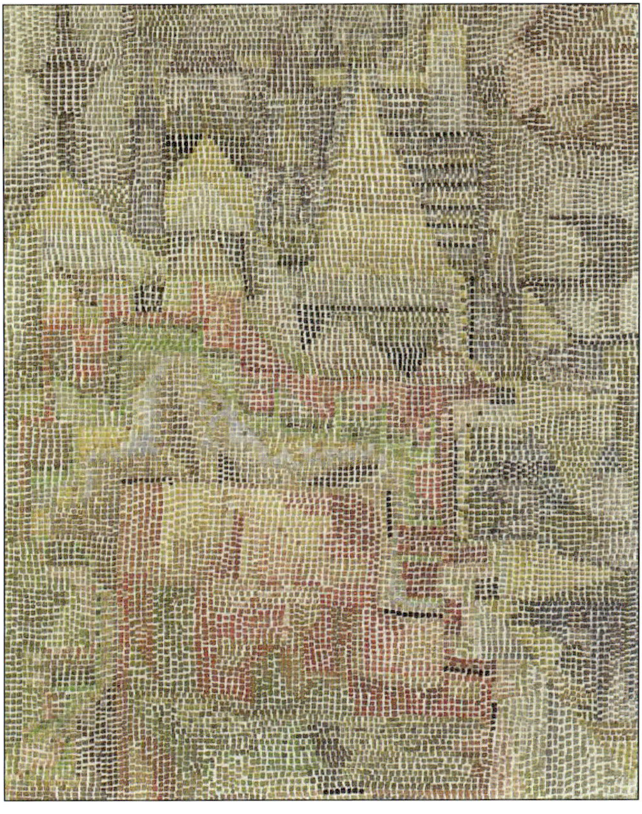

Plate 53

THE LAST MERCENARY

1932, The Barnes Foundation, Philadelphia

32.7 x 21 cm, Watercolor on wove paper; artist-mounted to paperboard

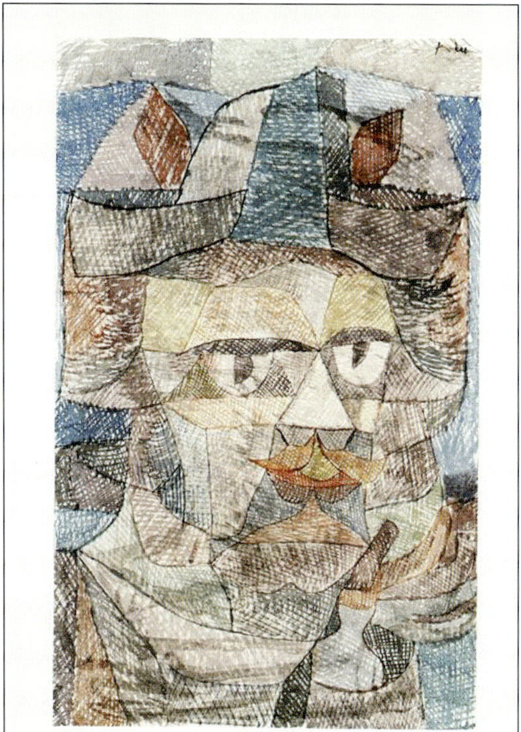

Plate 54

WALK IN THE ORIENT

1932, The Barnes Foundation, Philadelphia

21 x 33 cm, Watercolor on prepared paper; artist-mounted to paperboard

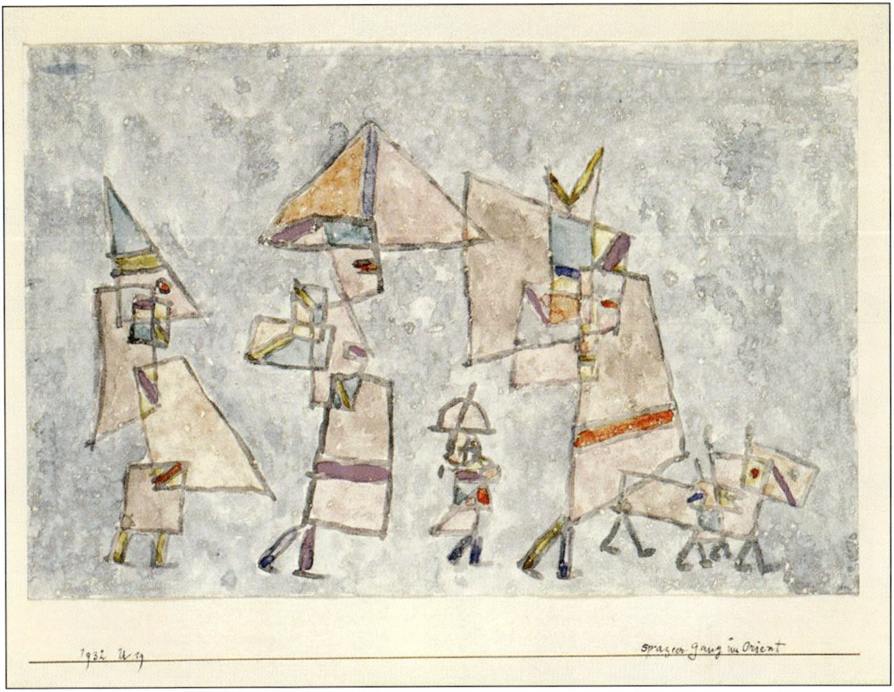

Plate 55

AD PARNASSUM

1932, Kunstmuseum Bern, Switzerland
100 x 126 cm, Oil on canvas

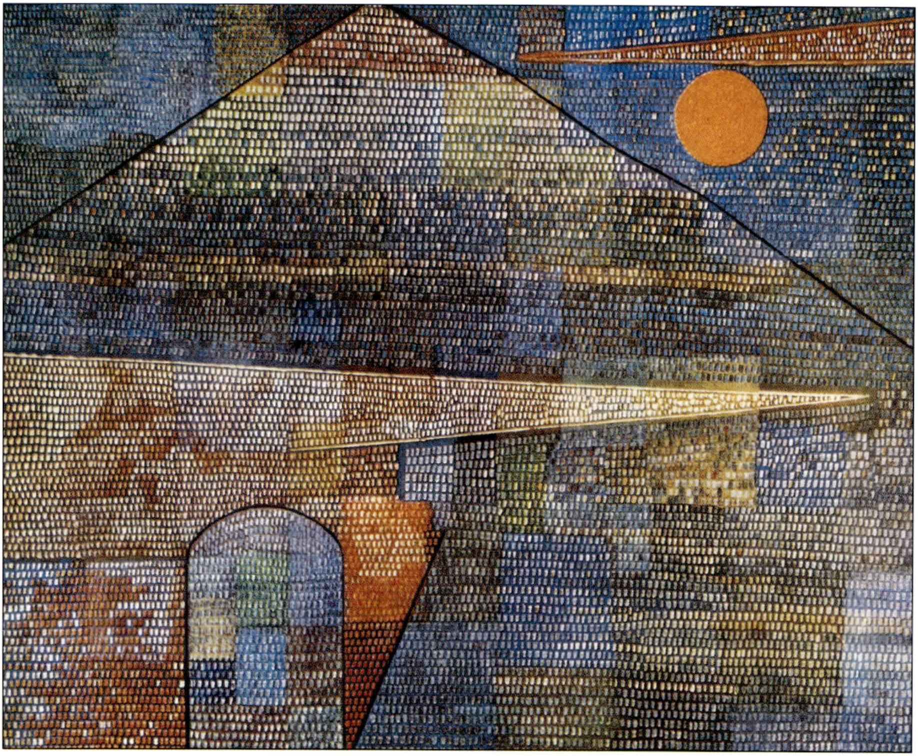

MASK OF FEAR

1932, Museum of Modern Art, New York City
100.4 x 57.1 cm, Oil on burlap

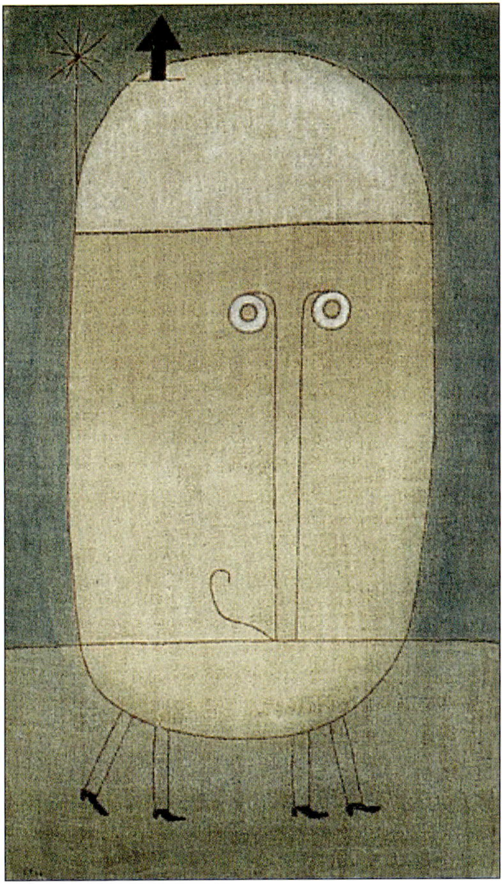

Plate 57

EQUALS INFINITY

1932, Museum of Modern Art, New York City
51.4 x 68.3 cm, Oil on canvas mounted on wood

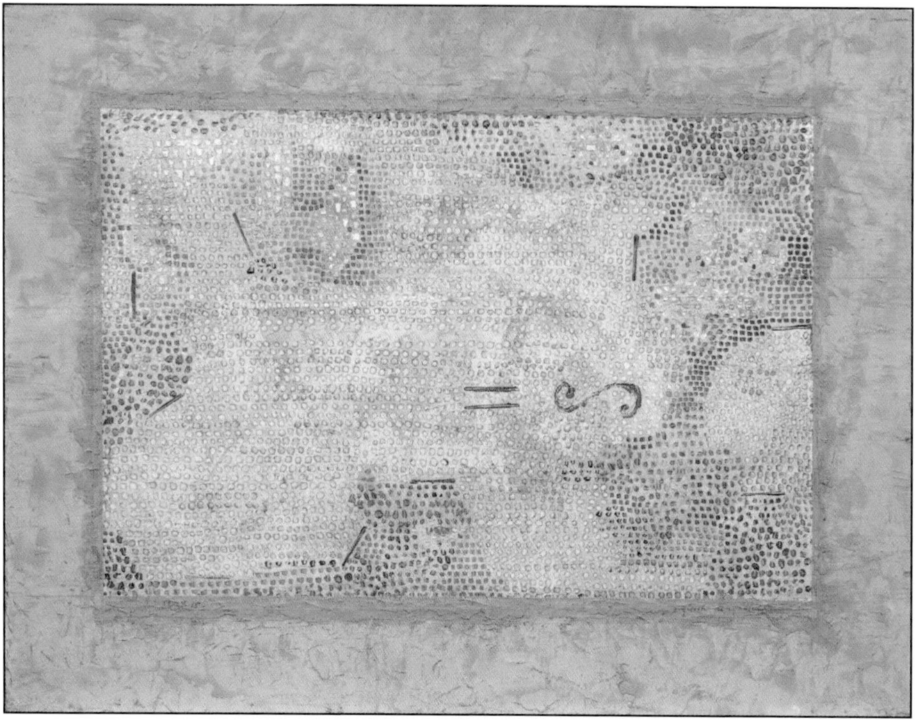

IN THE MAGIC MIRROR

1934, The Art Institute of Chicago
66 x 50 cm, Oil on canvas, on board

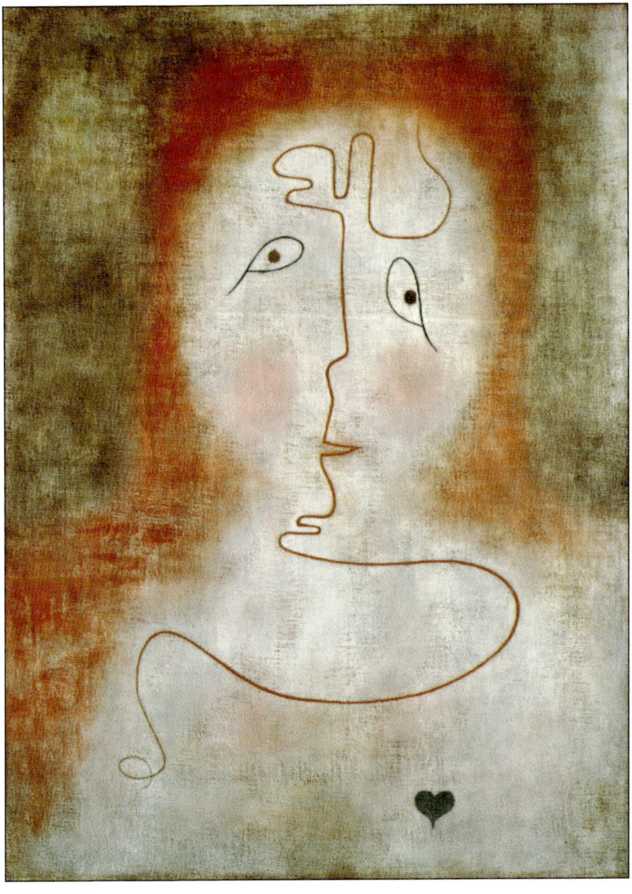

Plate 59

WALPURGIS NIGHT

1935, Tate Modern, London

50.8 x 47 cm, Gouache on fabric on plywood

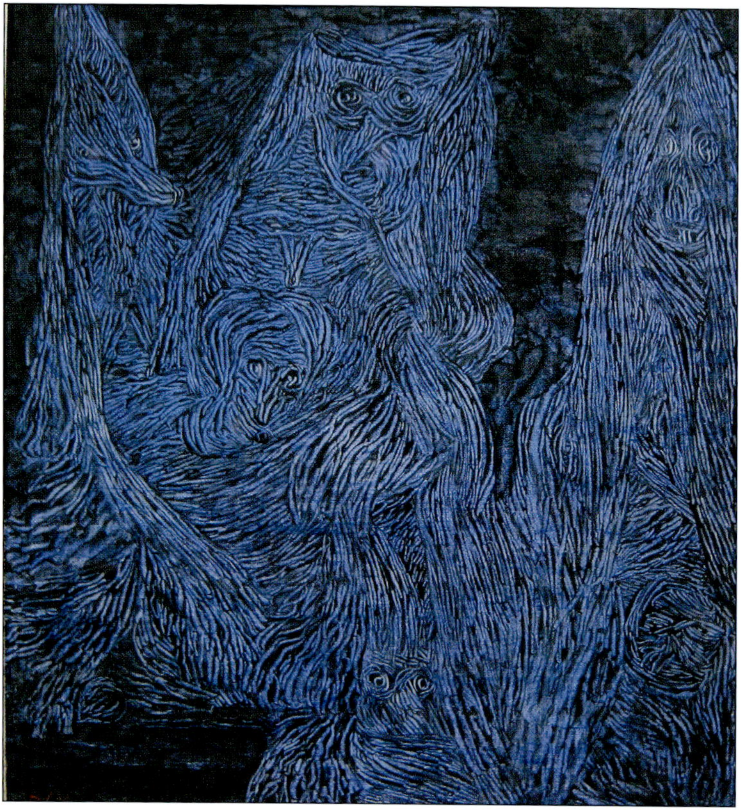

LADY DEMON

1935, Zentrum Paul Klee, Bern, Switzerland

150 x 100 cm, Oil and watercolor on primed burlap on cardboard; original frame

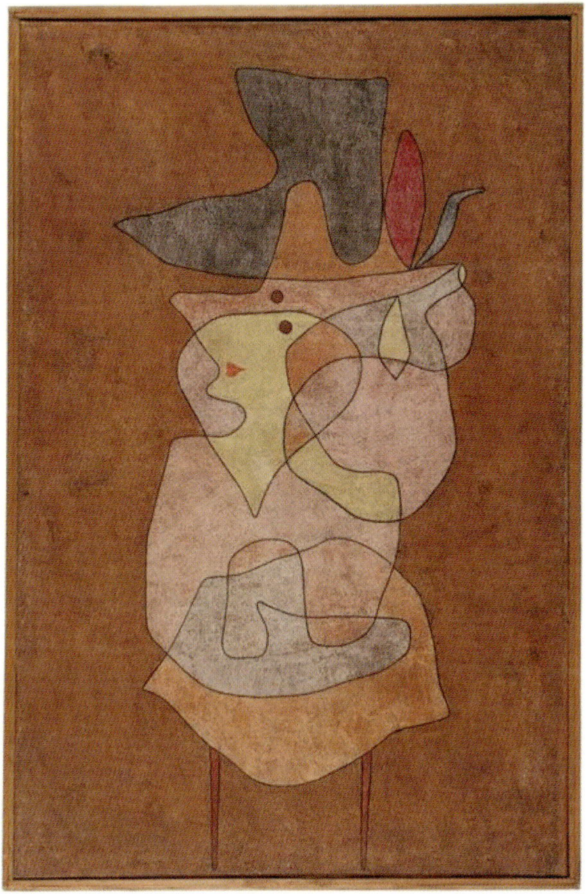

Plate 61

AFTER THE FLOOD

1936, Beyeler Foundation, Riehen, Switzerland

47.9 x 62.6 cm, Colored paste and watercolor on Ingres paper on cardboard

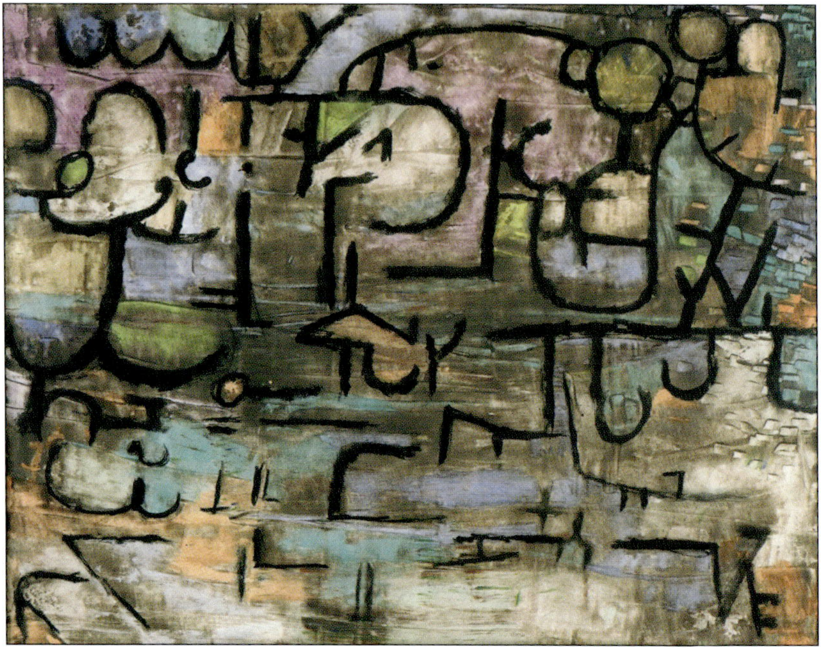

SOUTHERN GARDENS

1937, Beyeler Foundation, Riehen, Switzerland
25.5 x 30.5 cm, Colored paste on wrapping paper on cardboard

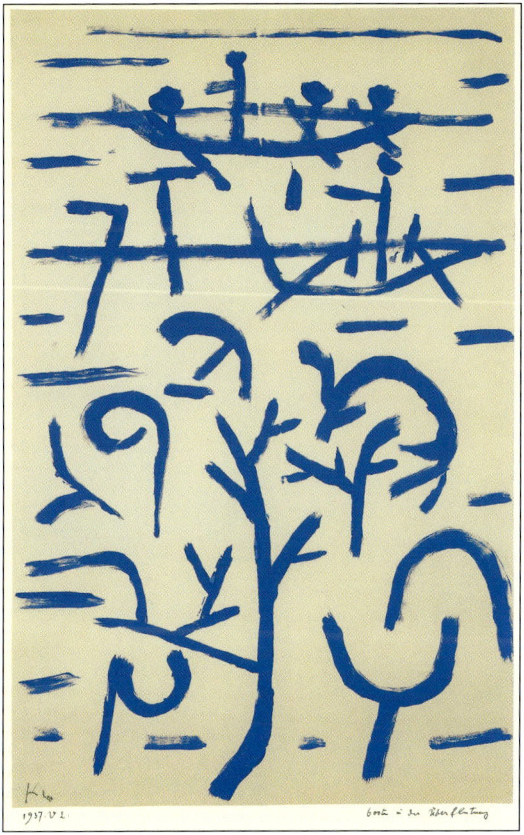

Plate 63

SIGNS IN YELLOW

1937, Beyeler Foundation, Riehen, Switzerland

83.5 x 50.3 cm, Pastel on cotton on colored paste on burlap on stretcher

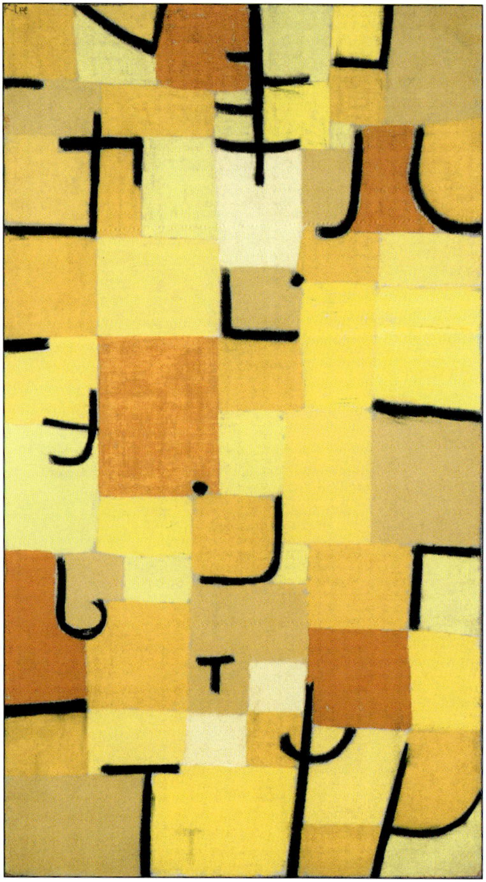

BLUE NIGHT

1937, Kunstmuseum Basel, Switzerland
50.5 x 76.5 cm, Pastel on cotton, pasted on jute; original frame strips

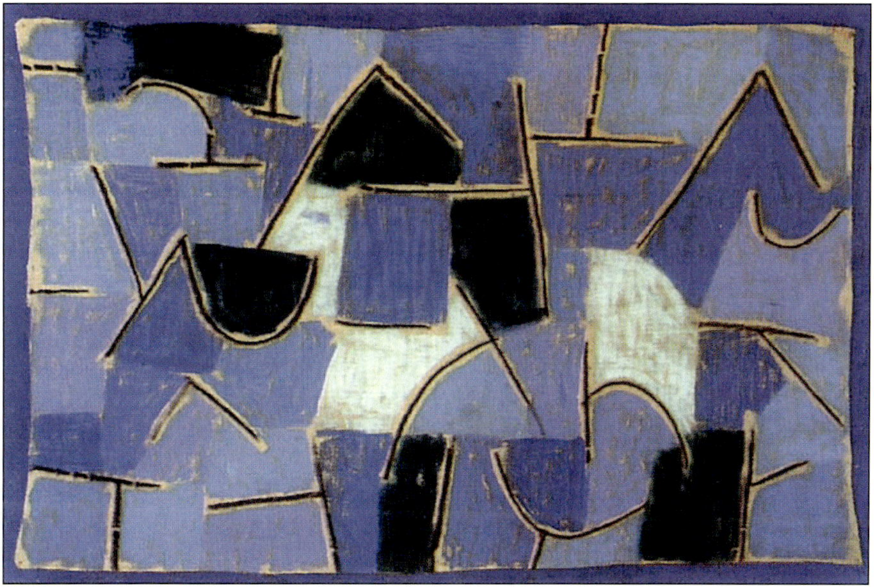

BLADES

1938, Beyeler Foundation, Riehen, Switzerland
50 x 35 cm, Colored paste on paper on cardboard

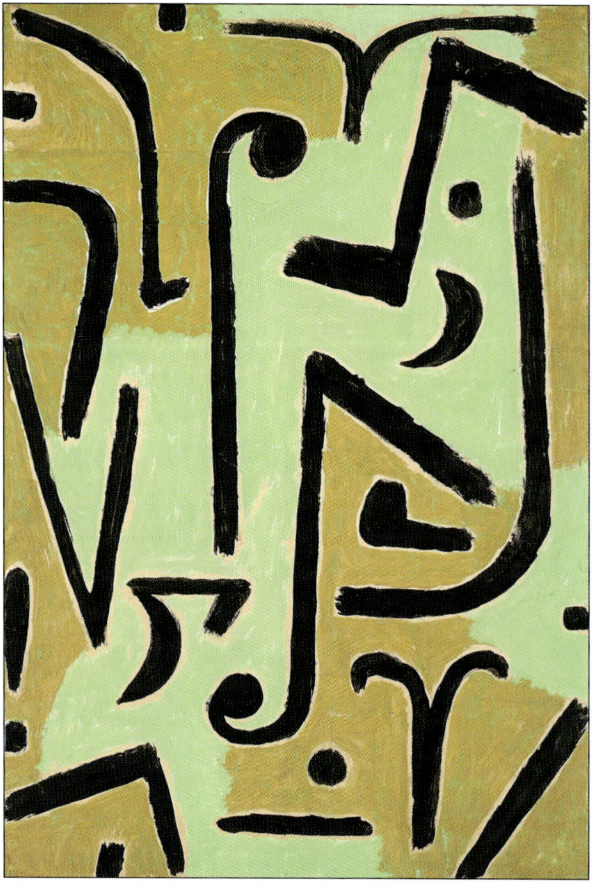

FOREST WITCHES

1938, Beyeler Foundation, Riehen, Switzerland
99 x 74 cm, Oil on paper on burlap

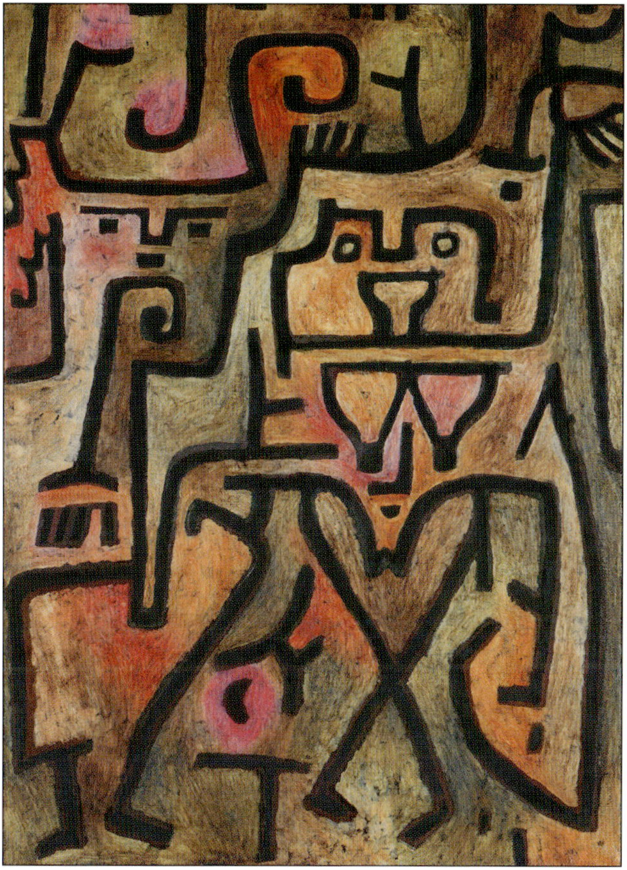

Plate 67

A WOMAN FOR GODS

1938, Beyeler Foundation, Riehen, Switzerland

44.3 x 60.5 cm, Colored paste and watercolor on wrapping paper on cardboard

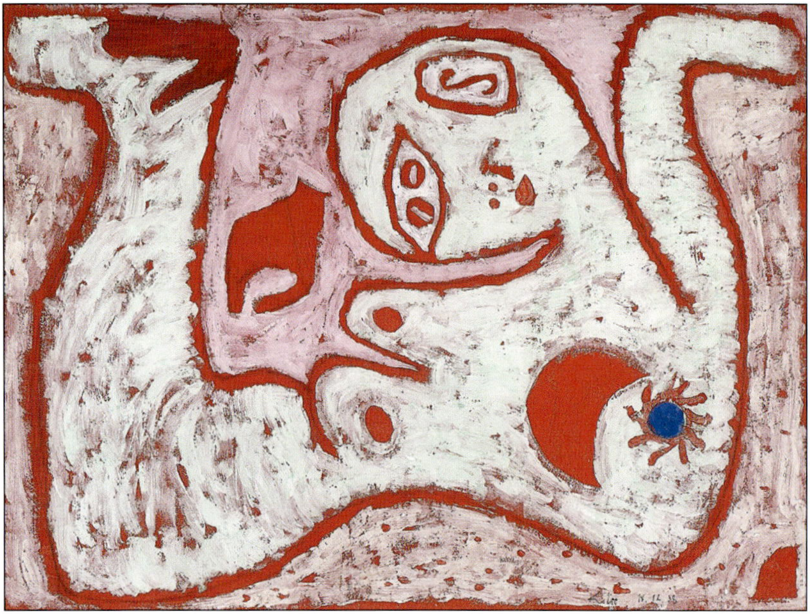

HEROIC STROKES OF THE BOX

1938, Musuem of Modern Art, New York City
73 x 53 cm, Pigmented paste on newspaper on dyed cloth on board in artist's frame (frame not shown)

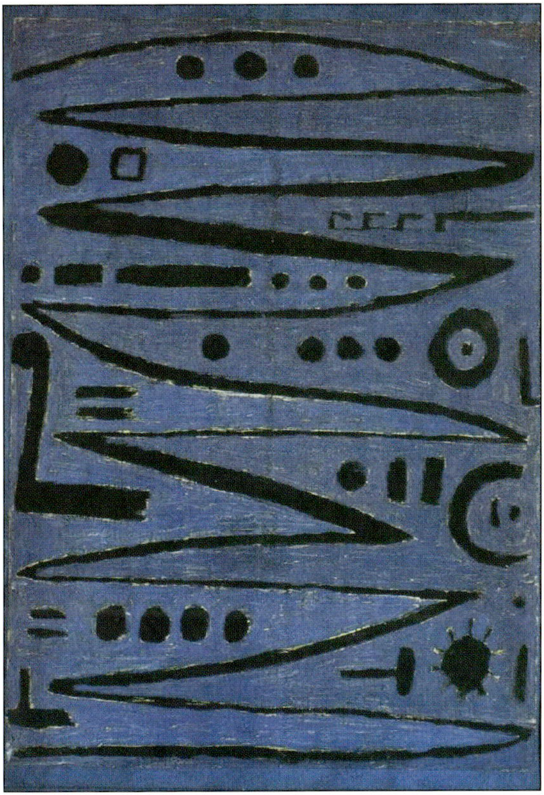

THE VASE

1938, Beyeler Foundation, Riehen, Switzerland
88 x 54.5 cm, Oil on burlap on burlap

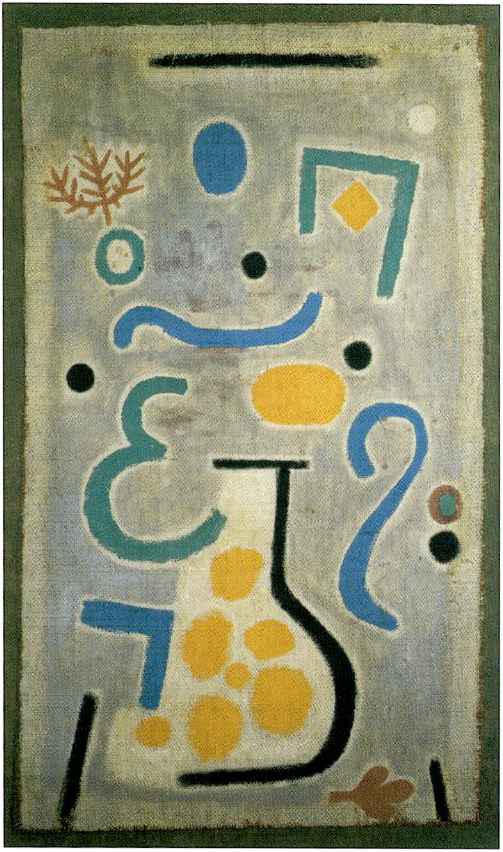

OH! THESE RUMORS!

1938, Beyeler Foundation, Riehen, Switzerland
75.5 x 55 cm, Tempera and oil on burlap

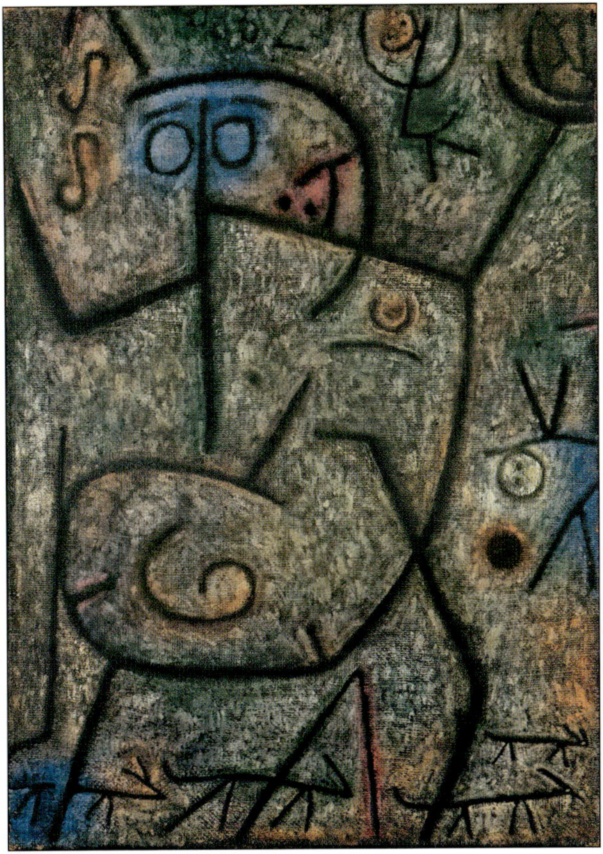

Plate 71

AN ALLEGORY OF PROPAGANDA

1939, Victoria and Albert Museum, London
50 x 38 cm, Tempera and oil on brown wrapping paper

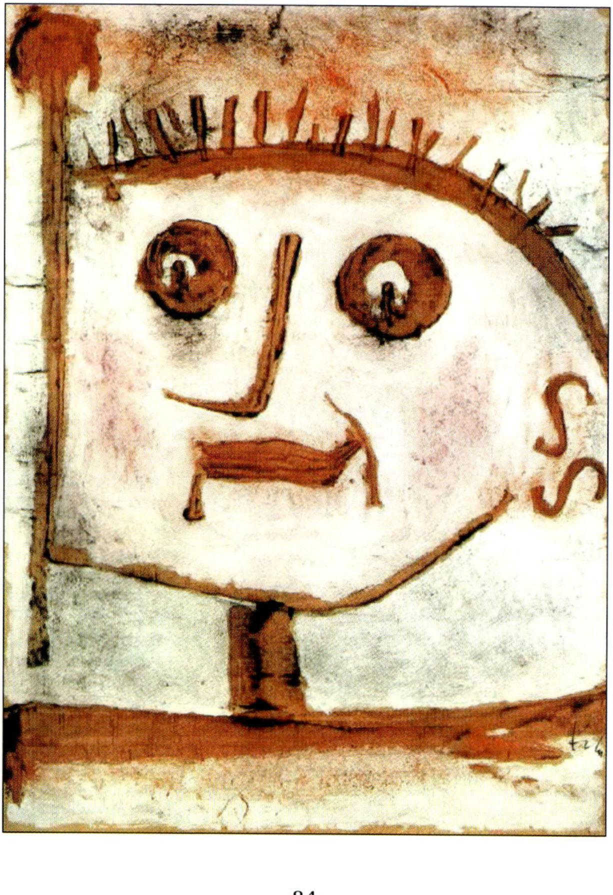

A GATE

1939, Beyeler Foundation, Riehen, Switzerland
31.6 x 14 cm, Tempera on Ingres paper on cardboard

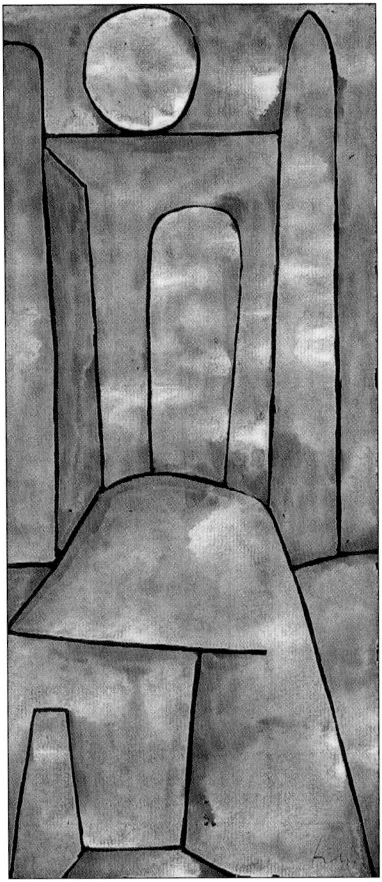

Plate 73

ANGEL, STILL FEMALE

1939, Zentrum Paul Klee, Bern, Switzerland

41.7 x 29.4 cm, Chalk on primed paper on cardboard

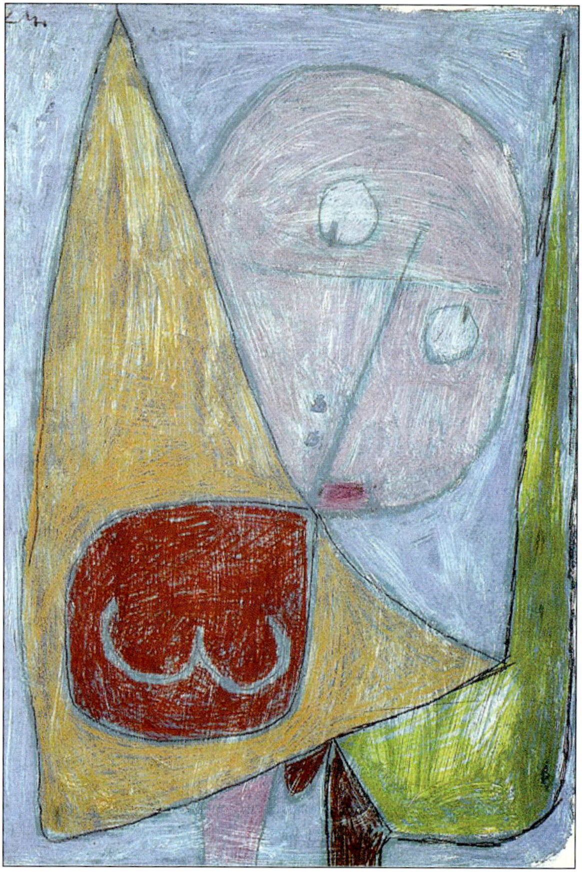

BLUE BIRD PUMPKIN

1939, The Metropolitan Museum of Art, New York City
27.9 x 43.2 cm, Gouache on paper

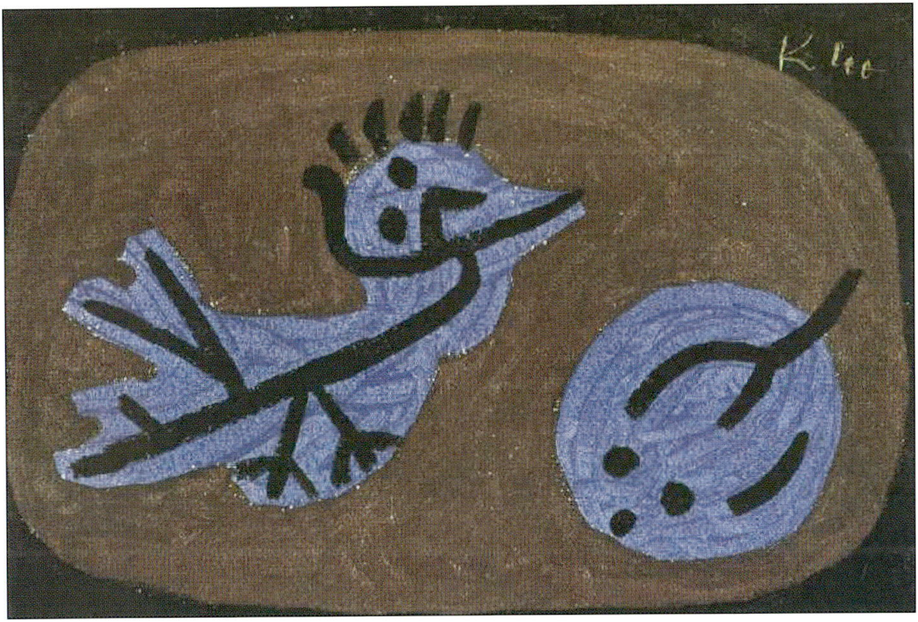

Plate 75

PARK OF IDOLS

1939, Zentrum Paul Klee, Bern, Switzerland
32.7 x 20.8 cm, Watercolor on primed paper on cardboard

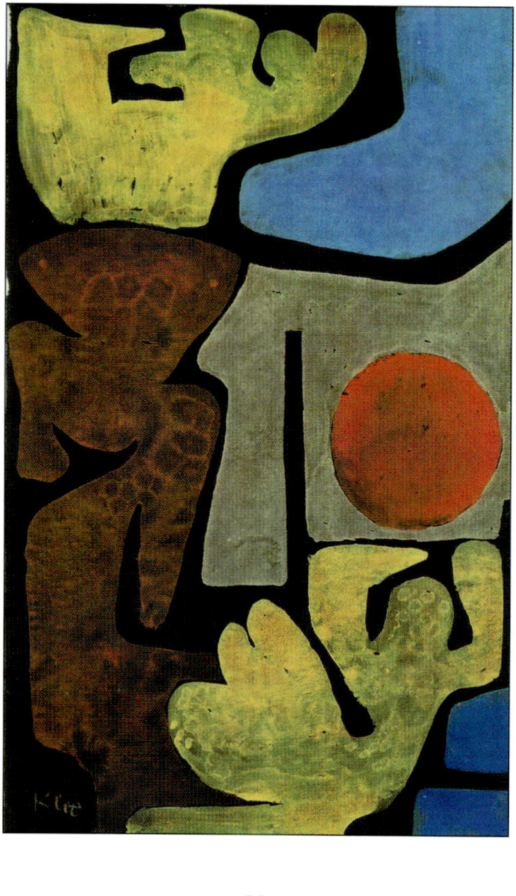

HISTORIC GROUND

1939, The Barnes Foundation, Philadelphia
26.8 x 22.2 cm, Watercolor with graphite underdrawing on wove paper; artist-mounted to paperboard

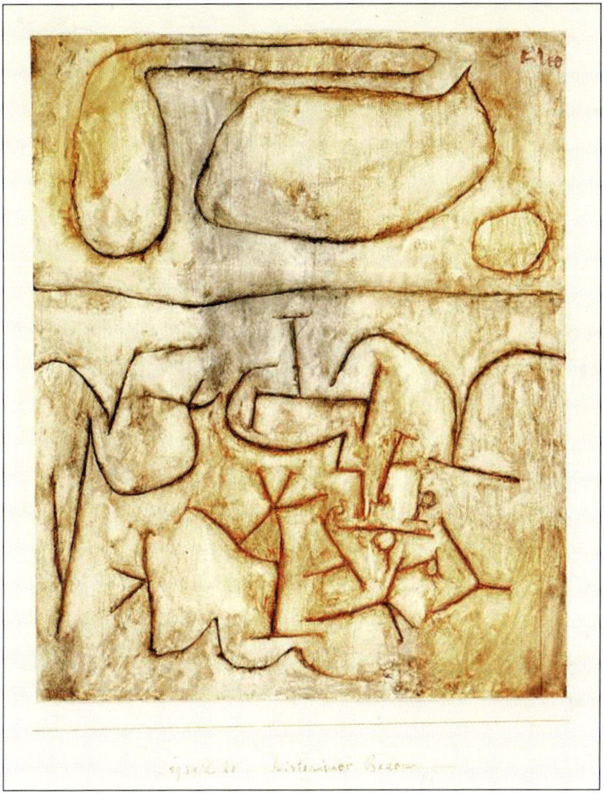

Plate 77

OUTBREAK OF FEAR

1939, Zentrum Paul Klee, Bern, Switzerland

63.5 x 48.1 cm, Watercolor on primed paper on cardboard

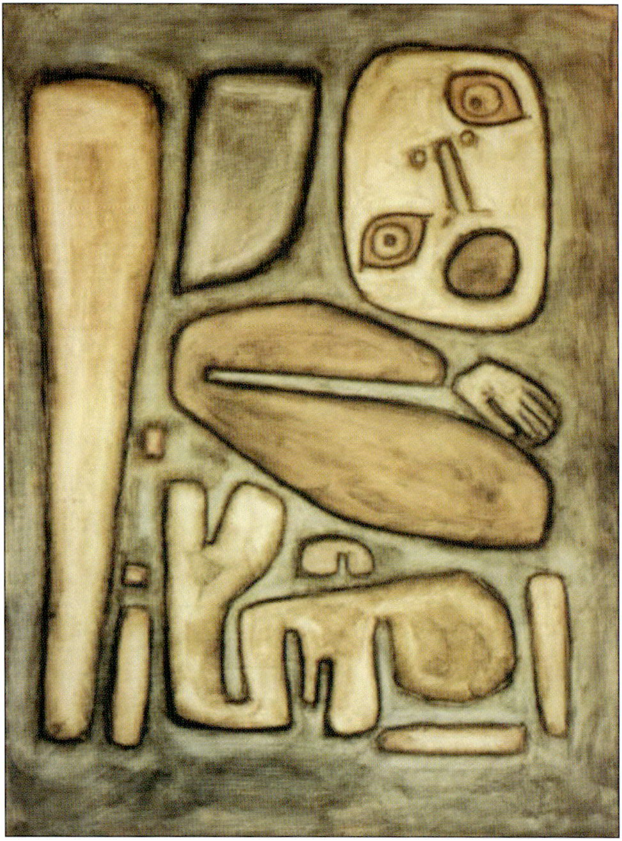

UNTITLED (CAPTIVE)

c. 1940, Beyeler Foundation, Riehen, Switzerland
55.2 x 50.1 cm, Oil and colored paste on primed burlap on burlap

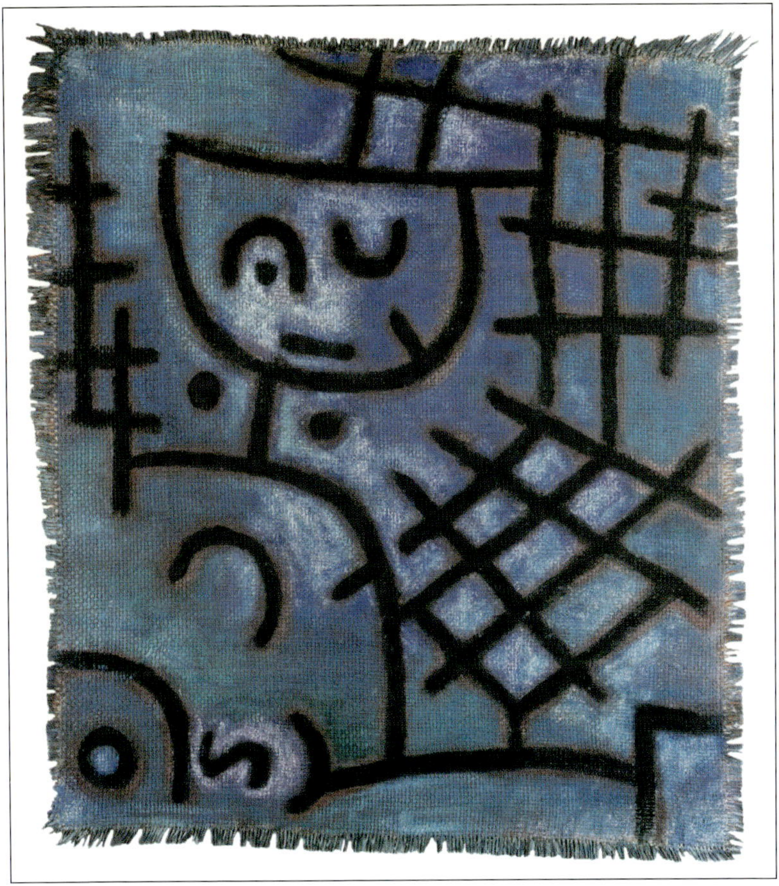

Plate 79

MUD-WOODLOUSE-FISH

1940, Beyeler Foundation, Riehen, Switzerland

34 x 53.5 cm, Colored paste and grease crayon on newspaper on cardboard

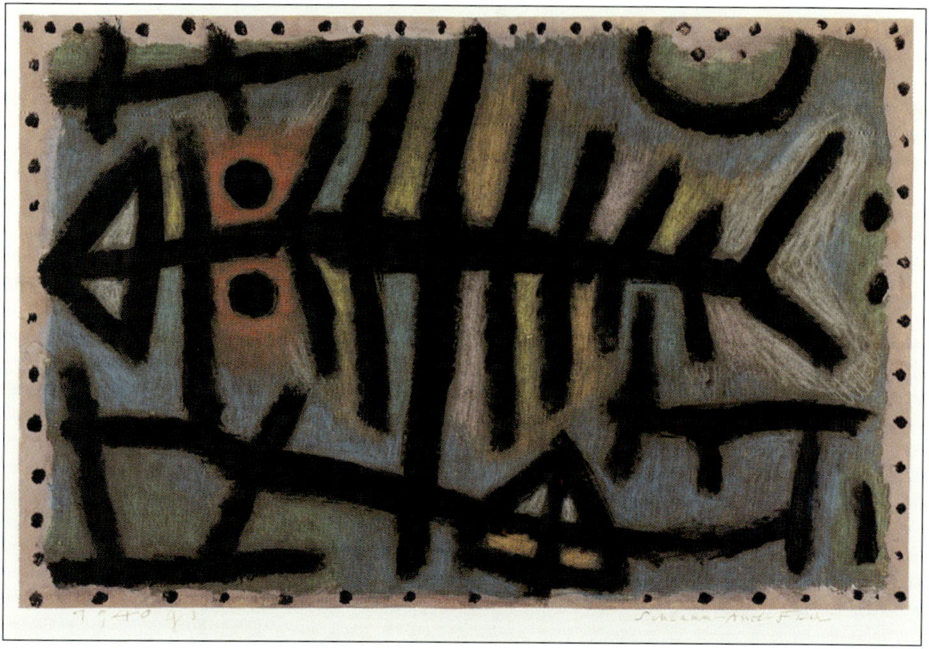

THE TRAVELING CIRCUS

c. 1940, São-Paulo Museum of Art
63.6 x 49.3 cm, Lithograph

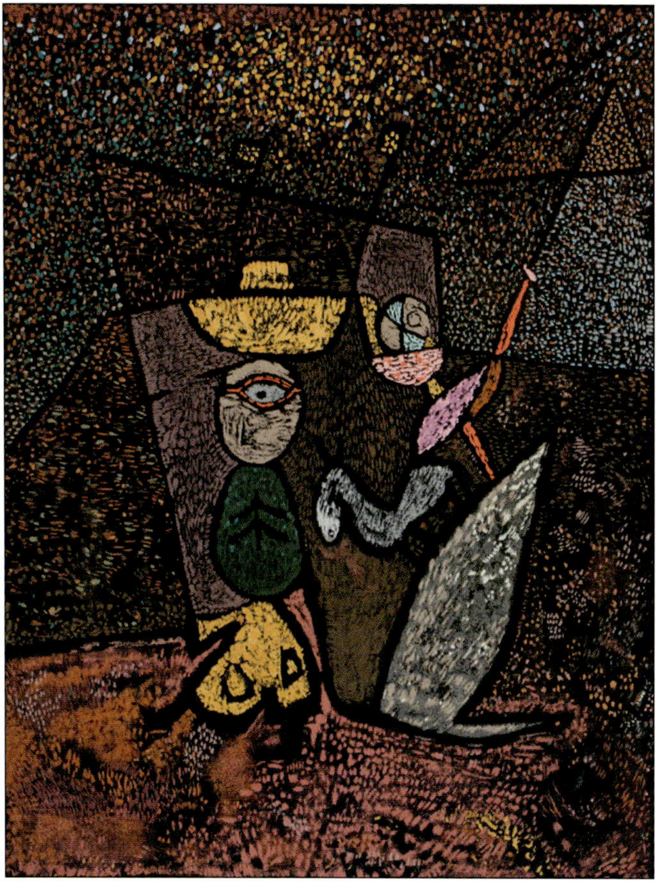

Plate 81

DEATH AND FIRE

1940, Zentrum Paul Klee, Bern, Switzerland

46.7 × 44.6 cm, Oil and colored paste on burlap; original frame

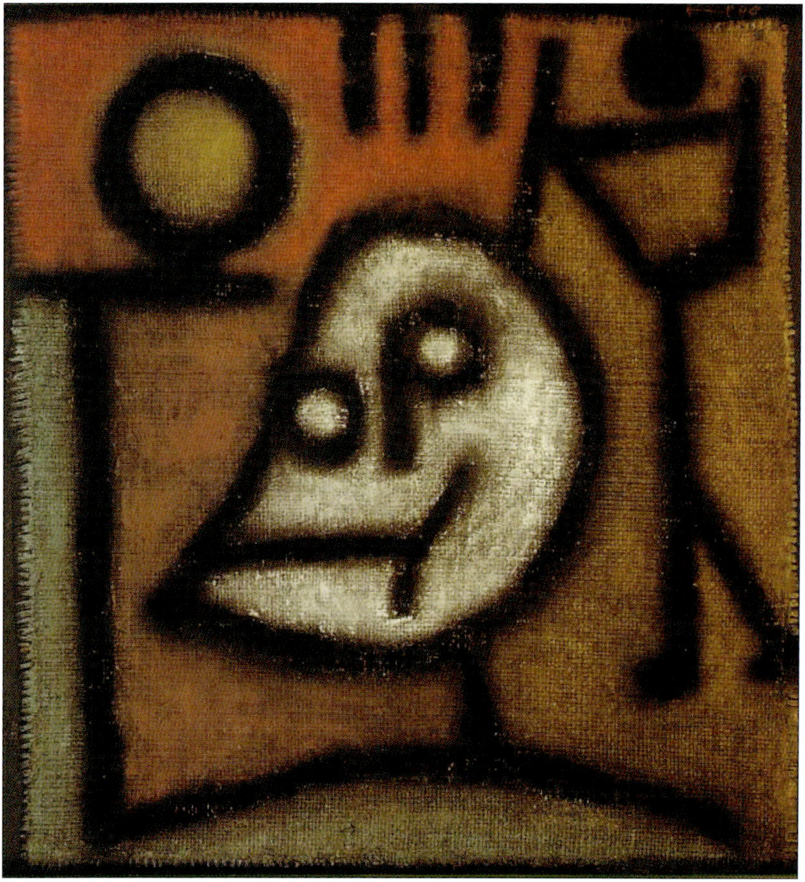

UNTITLED (LAST STILL LIFE)

1940, Zentrum Paul Klee, Bern, Switzerland

100 x 80.5 cm, Oil on canvas

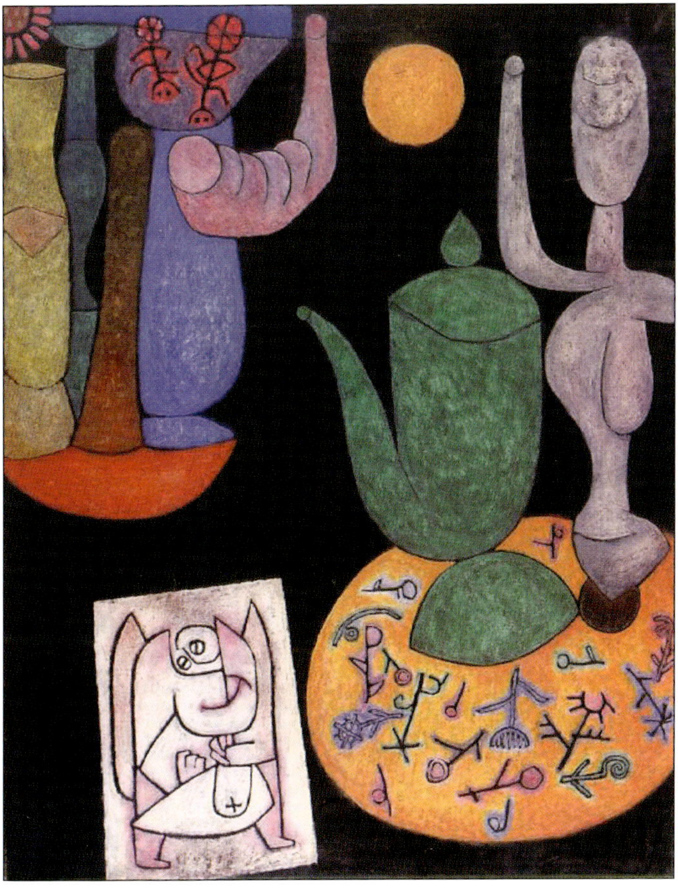

INDEX